# SHOW ME THE HARMONY

# SHOW ME THE HARMONY

## Discover the true superpower of new-age leaders!

Mark Worthington

First published 2023 by Mark Worthington.

Second revised edition 2024

www.mark-worthington.com

Copyright © Mark Worthington 2023, 2024

The moral rights of the author have been asserted.

All rights reserved. No part of this book may be reproduced or transmitted by any person or entity, including internet search engines or retailers (including, but not restricted to, Google and Amazon), in any form or by any means, electronic or mechanical, including photocopying (except under the statutory exceptions provisions of the Australian Copyright Act 1968), recording, scanning or by any information storage and retrieval system without the prior written permission of the author.

The author expressly prohibits any entity from using this publication in any manner for purposes of training artificial intelligence (AI) technologies to generate text, including without limitation technologies that are capable of generating works in the same style or genre as this publication. The author reserves all rights to license uses of this work for generative AI training and development of machine learning language models.

Because of the dynamic nature of the internet, any web addresses or links contained in this book may have changed since publication and may no longer be valid. The author of this book does not dispense medical advice or prescribe the use of any technique as a form of treatment for physical, emotional, or medical problems without the advice of a physician, either directly or indirectly. The intent of the author is only to offer information of a general nature to help you in your quest for emotional and spiritual wellbeing. In the event you use any of the information in this book for yourself, which is your constitutional right, the author assumes no responsibility for your actions.

Cover design by Julia Kuris, Designerbility designerbility.com.au

Internal design by Zena Shapter, zenashapter.com

Diagrams and Pictures by Bill Shapter, posbycheckout.com

# CONTENTS

**INTRODUCTION**    9
    The Pathway to Infinite Possibility Awaits    9

**CHAPTER 1: Tuning into a More Natural Way of Life**    35
    1.1 The Code of Happiness Applied to Collectives    35
    1.2 Harmonies at Play in a Wonderful Way    37
    1.3 Nature Plays One-Song    42

**CHAPTER 2: What Tunes are We Choosing to Play?**    53

**CHAPTER 3: Are Leaders Born or Created?**    62

**CHAPTER 4: Advanced Leadership Tools to Inspire Possibility**    66
    4.1 Leadership is Not Management, It's Art    66
    4.2 Aligning Expectations With Outcomes    72
    4.3 The Evolving Energy of Our Conductors    78
    4.4 Why Do We Ignore the Golden Rule?    86
    4.5 The Grand Distortion of Money and Profit    89
    4.6 Shepherds Take the Higher Ground    98
    4.7 Embracing the Energy of Fear    104
    4.8 Unity Over Separation    116
    4.9 Who Cares Wins!    121
    4.10 Encouraging Both Forms of Intelligence    124
    4.11 Standing for Transformation, Not Information    128
    4.12 Communicating for Trust    131

| | |
|---|---|
| 4.13 The Responsibility to Believe in Autonomy | 135 |
| 4.14 Being Energised, Not Timed | 136 |
| 4.15 Balancing the 4 Ps | 138 |
| 4.16 Reshaping the Meaning of Success | 144 |
| 4.17 Embracing the Inevitability of Rebirths | 146 |
| 4.18 Relaxing into Who We Are | 150 |
| 4.19 A Chance to Self-Reflect | 152 |
| 4.20 Practical Aspects of Becoming an Advanced Leader | 155 |

| | |
|---|---|
| **CHAPTER 5: Core Traits of Highly Evolved Collectives** | **160** |
| 5.1 Rediscovering the Purity of Life | 160 |
| 5.2 Becoming More | 168 |
| 5.3 The Forgotten Power of the Sphere | 171 |
| 5.4 Redefining the Concept of Winning and Losing | 184 |
| 5.5 The Need for Better Questions | 194 |
| 5.6 We Can't Handle the Truth | 209 |
| 5.7 The Solidarity of Truth, Trust, and Purpose | 212 |
| 5.8 A Chance to Self-Reflect | 214 |

| | |
|---|---|
| **CHAPTER 6: Stepping Stones to Harmony** | **217** |
| **CHAPTER 7: Our Opportunity to Transform Together** | **238** |
| **CHAPTER 8: Concluding Remarks** | **245** |
| 8.1 Can the Wise Leaders Please Step Forward! | 245 |
| **APPENDIX I: Checklist for Evolving Leaders** | **249** |
| **APPENDIX II: 30 Mantras** | **259** |
| **APPENDIX III: Our 22 Core Limiting Beliefs Re-played** | **263** |
| **Acknowledgements** | **269** |
| **About the Author** | **271** |

*This book is dedicated to those who taught me much during my professional career, and brought me opportunities to expand and grow, both personally and professionally.*

*I was fortunate to have served in some highly valued organisations with leading practitioners, many of whom showed an unwavering commitment to the organisations they served. Each and every one of them taught me much.*

*I have also lived in and experienced various sophisticated societies that helped me to witness how leaders all over the world have responded to events and crises.*

*I honour all our leaders, past and present, for having the fortitude to carry the responsibilities that leadership entails. As is often said, it can be lonely at the top. Although, does it need to be? And is there really a top?*

*I also honour my five children who gave me great motivation to be the best I could be throughout my changing career. Their support was and continues to be amazing.*

*I was never a perfect leader, but I strived to improve continuously in every experience. I loved creating transformation through the powers of love and truth, and accordingly this was my leadership passion. It's a passion that continues to burn bright inside me, and I doubt it will ever be dimmed or extinguished.*

*This book is written to assist our future leaders to expand their awareness beyond that experienced by the generations of leaders before them. I dedicate it to these 'new-age' leaders, regardless of their walks of life, for being prepared to step forward for the benefit of all who choose to follow. Our latent possibilities will grow from the foundations these brave men and women establish. Evolution is our natural state, and the principles of evolution apply to leadership as much as any other aspect of life. Like a lighthouse on a dark night, these evolving leaders will shine a light on what is possible as our future unfolds, and as we encounter ongoing change.*

*Evolution involves a gradual yet constant series of transformations. This is how nature works. And we are very much a part of nature.*

*Our future depends heavily on how our leaders will cope with and lead us through the ongoing disruptions we are sure to experience in the future. Great possibilities will arise once we learn to create through unity not separation, collaboration not competition, and the powers of love and truth.*

Mark Worthington
Author

# INTRODUCTION

## The Pathway to Infinite Possibility Awaits

I have written this book to help create a better future for all of us. It has been inspired by my own journey of transformation, my experiences in the business world and my personal life. It embodies what I understand about the potential that awaits us, if we are prepared to consider new ways of leading collectives to help them expand and transform.

After reading this book, I hope you will appreciate the possibilities its ideas present to our thinking as a society, as well to you as an individual. It's time for leadership to evolve and reshape our world! And we all get to lead in some way, even if it's just to lead our own lives.

Our world is in a constant state of flux and how we handle inevitable change is of critical importance. I therefore hope to offer a blueprint of leadership significantly different to what is exhibited in most current walks of life. That doesn't mean some leaders aren't already aligned with the concepts I espouse; it just means they are in the minority.

Regardless of your own level of alignment with my views, in order to fully consider the impact that leadership has on our lives, and to consider how it can be enhanced, you will need to keep an open mind, and develop a willingness to step forward with others to engage in new paradigms of leadership. Love and truth, not fear and manipulation, are the natural forces we need in great abundance.

However, our society is highly conditioned to accept many 'normal' or well-worn practices that are based on fear and expectation. Our conditioned minds lead us to specific forms of behaviour as a collective, which will of course meet our expectations because we are accustomed to them – but are they what we truly want?

We need to look deeply behind the behaviours and actions we exhibit as leaders, and examine them critically, for behind every action could be a conscious or subconscious belief that we have been conditioned to hold true. Until these beliefs are identified and acknowledged, it doesn't matter how many laws or rules we create to mandate behaviours or values in our collectives, the current paradigms will persist.

From my experience, little is really understood or discussed of the beliefs that drive organisational or societal behaviours. Under pressure, it is often said that we revert to type – in other words, our beliefs lead us in a certain way when 'the heat is on'. Is it any wonder then that our normal behavioural standards take precedence in an emergency? Yet this is when leaders need to be at their most open-minded, dynamic and aware.

The world today is full of many growing societies, communities and organisations, each becoming increasingly complex. Even families in many cultures are witnessing growing complexities. The likelihood of disruption is thus more and more likely. We need to face this, not hide from it. Disruption is best faced through inclusion, not exclusion, for we need each other to thrive, not just survive. At its very core, we are one big family, alive together.

So, let me take you on a journey into new possibilities, and a new way of creating through unity, love, and truth.

## Many Microcosms Create a Macrocosm

The world is an aggregation of individuals, their combined experiences and actions. Collective happiness is therefore directly influenced by the happiness of individuals, and vice versa. We may try to blame 'the world' for our less-than-ideal situations, and for the collective pain it may produce; but surely we must also then recognise that we are all a part of the problem, to differing degrees, even if it's just through accepting what is.

The good news is, this also means we can all be a part of the solution! This is an exciting prospect when we open to it fully. We are all here to grow and learn, individually and collectively. We can each make changes that will reflect outwards like a beam of light, influencing the whole.

I myself have been a microcosm of the macrocosm, swinging from mastery to misery at times. Yet the greatest barrier to reaching my full potential was always my own lack of self-awareness. I had to rebuild myself from the inside out on a number of occasions, for my light had dimmed out of ignorance, and because without expanding your self-awareness as a human being, your growth will largely be limited to copying others. Self-awareness comes from the ability to self-reflect and is blocked in those who see themselves as not needing to expand. Self-reflection is a trait every advanced leader should want and expect in their team. However, it's the leader who needs to model this, so others in the team feel that they have permission to do the same.

A key step is to simply be aware of our propensity to be self-righteous. When we experience something we don't like, we often judge the people involved, criticise them, then distance ourselves from the problem. Our egos want to take the credit when something goes well, but we blame our challenging times on: others, the environment, or sheer bad luck. Once blame has been established, we get to elevate ourselves, because we feel that we are in the right, and free of blame. We can walk away and be holier than thou. Sound familiar? Through righteousness, we can all think we are superior at times.

It's easy to criticise, but much harder to look within ourselves for attributions of blame, and our leaders are often large and open targets for it. Sometimes it doesn't seem to matter that our leaders are the only ones willing to put their hands up, to step into the challenge of taking charge and assisting the collective. It doesn't seem to matter that we all know leadership can be an extremely difficult task, fraught with the challenge of trying to see the totality of things, even when it can be almost impossible to do so.

Yet if we can become aware of how acutely self-righteousness blinds us, we will be able to reflect more logically and reasonably on the issues that both the world and its leaders face, then contribute to resolutions, paving the way to communal advancement. Most leaders are simply just doing their best – and what more can we really ask of a person than for them to do their best?

In my book *Where Your Happiness Hides*, I explored how I personally came to witness my deepest reflection in the mirror. Self-reflection allowed me to see what I was not, and what I could be. Personal loss gave me the power to self-reflect, and to go on an incredible journey of transformation. I saw just how influential simple beliefs were in creating the unhappy life I was living. Until I addressed those beliefs, I stood no chance of changing my life for the better. I needed to stop leading myself into problems, through my lack of self-awareness, and it was only when I witnessed my need to evolve through a lens of self-compassion that my life changed for the better.

Self-reflection is the greatest architect of self-awareness, and is available to everyone, even collectives of people. Indeed, our lack of awareness is at the root of our core issues as a race, and this has been developed through centuries of conditioned thinking, and often painful experiences and memories that are deeply embedded in us. Our leaders have unfortunately allowed our collective consciousness to manifest into this reality, and for many it is not a wonderful experience. If only we could think less, and feel more, we could create what our hearts truly desire. Our hearts know what we want. Our minds only *think* they do!

Using me as a 'guinea pig', here are a few of the parallels I have witnessed. I was the microcosm, society the macrocosm. I have been far from perfect, but I now cherish this for what it has taught me.

| My Microcosm | Our Macrocosm |
|---|---|
| Broken relationships – two divorces | A legalistic world, searching for blame |
| Self-protection and projection | Wars, conflicts, image management |
| Financial losses | Economic instability |
| Significant health problems | Diseases (eg. cancer, heart disease) |
| Stress | Social distress and unrest |
| A need to win | A competitive society |
| A focus on materialism, not learning | Consumerism on a mass scale |

Once I saw my plight, however, I did not give up on myself, but instead realised that I was in fact causing my own issues. I took to owning those issues, and vowed to change by growing my self-awareness and focussing my energies through the higher consciousness arising from within me. I allowed my broken heart to come back together, soft, light, and strong. As a society we can do the same. It's the natural state we truly desire. Together we can put forth a new way of viewing life, and an advanced way of redefining the concepts of leadership. The two go hand-in-hand!

In discarding the concept of blame altogether, we can also dispense with the need for forgiveness, and embrace understanding instead. For the sake of any leaders who have stepped into the lion's den, we must also acknowledge how difficult it is to succeed once inside that den, with judgement and blame being served up on a never-ending platter. We must approach this with compassion, and from a place of love. Too few have made this journey, but it can gather momentum as we collectively question our circumstances.

Eventually, we will be able to again put our faith in leaders, though they may look and appear different to those we have become accustomed to, because they may speak and behave very differently. But we will identify these new shepherds, for we need them to help us find new pastures, and to steer our flock to greater abundance. Their willingness to embrace higher states of awareness and to stand for love, truth, and unity will be their defining feature.

Collectives led by unaware leaders simply cannot flow to the full extent possible. They are like an orchestra without a trained conductor – their harmonies will be less than ideal, and the audience and musicians will feel lesser for the experience. We need leaders who can stand for a shared purpose, for they live within their hearts first and foremost.

## The Power of Mistakes

Effective transformation is reliant on seeing the magic in mistakes and embracing them without harsh judgement. The advanced leaders we need will know this and embody it.

Whenever we make mistakes, or our decisions prove to be unsuccessful, there is great wisdom to be found in understanding why. There is no such thing as failure if we learn from what has gone wrong. It is here that much evolution is possible in our world. It can be as simple as redefining the meaning of success in our lives and orchestrating a new beginning with vibrancy.

Indeed, learning through the pain of mistakes can often be more productive than learning through success, since learning usually stops as soon as joy and celebrations begin – whether that is because we are meeting targets, exceeding expectations, or simply accomplishing goals.

Unfortunately, many individuals have become highly averse to failure of any kind, even if it is out of their control; for in this modern world losing our reputations can be seen as tragic.

But being afraid of failure can also prevent us from taking risks that might otherwise bring us success and adventure.

The key is to ask the right questions, especially in times of difficulty. This is where real magic can begin to weave its wonder. We are all at different stages of our journeys to self-awareness, so the simplest thing to do is acknowledge this, and help others further behind us on their own journeys.

Indeed, once the source of a mistake is understood, and we have grown through any available learning, the chance of repeating that mistake is much lower in the future. We can only grow from where we are, not from where we want to be; so if we adopt the perspective that our lives are a journey of love and learning, then there is much opportunity for us to grow as a collective of souls, and as individuals.

This can arise from the courage to own and confront our mistakes with the right questions and deep self-reflection, not self-deprecation. If this interests you, perhaps because you aspire to higher levels of leadership yourself, or because you seek to inspire leaders to evolve, I urge you to come on this journey to discover a more-aware you, and as a result help to create a more-aware community.

Remember, we are all leaders in our own way. At its very core, we all have lives to lead as individuals. But there are also leaders in and around us – in partnerships, families, schools, religious organisations, clubs, groups or tribes. Our shared happiness lies within these collectives, their evolution and transformation.

It won't be easy, but it will be enriching for those who choose to follow this path to new possibilities.

To put awareness another way: once we truly know, we can really grow. This is a quest I have much personal experience with and want to share with others. So, as you read this book, if you need further assistance with your transformation, or the transformation of a collective you lead, please don't hesitate to get in touch through my website at mark-worthington.com.

## The Infinite Power of Unification Over Separation

A core opportunity in our world is to embrace unity over separation.

Our world has become increasingly capable of contact in the last

100 years, largely as a result of new technologies. Yet, in a way, our world has become more disconnected than ever, and this is driving us to create a highly competitive world where only a fortunate few thrive, and the majority struggle. Much of this is subconscious, for we are programmed to expect to suffer and compete for limited resources. As a result, we often subconsciously embrace a separation mindset.

The Covid-19 pandemic temporarily put our separation mindset on steroids, as many of us were forced into lockdowns within our homes. Now, many of us are choosing to work or study from home, reinforcing the challenges that leaders face to create unity in the wider world.

At the same time, this shift is inviting many of us to find greater autonomy, as we crave better balance in our lives. But where is the right balance between the interests of the individual and the collectives to which they belong? Even before the pandemic this was a huge challenge for humanity and particularly those leading us.

Every collective – whether it be a nation, society, corporation, family or group of people – is comprised of individuals, who are each different. Eight billion souls inhabit this planet, and no two are completely the same. Each of us has a separate identity and soul. Each of us has different wants and needs.

Yet all of these individuals exhibit very similar patterns of behaviour and ways of thinking, which are supported by commonly inherited belief structures, handed down from generation to generation. We are born the same way, we all age and die, and we all need certain core things to survive, like food, water, and shelter. We also all want to be loved, and to be noticed for who we are. We crave connection and recognition. As a general rule we want to fit in, to come together and form various teams. It is therefore imperative to our collective happiness that we recognise our innate need for collaboration and unity, so that we can function as best we can as a unified organism.

It makes no sense to compete so hard for everything as individuals, though we do with great vigour. At the end of the day, who really wins? The answer is: not many people!

Our hearts know that this is not the best way we can be in this experience of life. At our very core, we are all pure love, yet we allow fear to rule how we think. And at the very core of our fears, is the belief or suspicion that we only live once, and will die on this planet with only the things we can acquire or create, representing our legacy. We choose in many cases to seek love and self-esteem through owning things outside ourselves, rather than looking inward to find truth and joy. This has made us competitive consumers who can be overly self-focussed, rather than mindful of both our individual and collective well-being.

Imagine a world where our collective well-being takes centre stage in the light of self-awareness, and we constantly try to do more to grow this aspect of ourselves. It is often said that a great team will always beat a team of great players. We say this, but how many of us live this way in reality?

True unity is a great opportunity, and our future depends on it! It must replace separation as our key cornerstone if we are to thrive and evolve together. Inclusion, not exclusion, is a must-do way of being that we need to embrace further, with great intent. We need to acknowledge that we might have mistaken 'contact' for 'connection' in our lives.

Indeed, while new technologies have allowed us to achieve more contact with each other 24/7 across the globe, meaningful connection is lost when we compete and withdraw in a place of distrust. The difference between contact and connection is defined by one word: presence. When we are not able to be deeply present with ourselves, we cannot be present with each other.

The new-age leader has this presence, and is able to bring it to bear to create unity and connection where mere 'contact' once lived. And presence can only be found in one place – in the energy of love. It lives in our hearts, and only in our hearts.

## The Power of Letting Go

To change anything, we need to be able to witness with an open heart and mind what needs to be changed. This requires an eye to truth and a desire to embrace it positively.

However, opening up to any new possibility inevitably means letting go of what was and seemed normal, and this can be harder than it sounds. Our egos want to avoid pain, and to direct pain at others for perceived deficiencies. They see change as a risk, and attempt to hold us in the status quo. Accordingly, we all struggle to let go.

To raise our self-awareness and to make positive change, we need to provide space to embrace the next phase of our lives. Letting go gives us that space, to let new possibilities in. Genuine forgiveness is what allows this to flow and be felt. Self-forgiveness may also be needed, and this can be more challenging, for we are often our own greatest critics. Collectively, therefore, we must forgive ourselves for issues we see as unfortunate. This also means forgiving leaders whose decisions may have been instrumental in their creation, for most likely they did their best, given their level of awareness.

Forgiveness can also allow us to truly grow and transcend our issues by allowing enhanced awareness to bring forth solutions. It is a strong and certain passageway to experiencing true peace in our hearts. The first step is to overcome the energy of blame.

Gratitude is also a very powerful energy that can take us beyond our current paradigms. When we accept that everything occurring could be a gift, with a purpose, then we can see the value in its unfolding. This requires us to give greater credibility to learning and growing through experiences, rather than just being obsessed with outcomes and the need to achieve certain desires.

As is often said, the journey is half the fun. But we are not there yet! We won't be until we learn to let go.

## Our Opportunity to Evolve Through Self-Awareness

Our world has so much potential to transform and evolve, to create new possibilities for all.

Evolution has gone from being a concept expressed by futurists and scientists to an imperative we can no longer put in the laps of future generations. We need to embrace the concept right now, in our own lives, so that through it we can find a greater state of harmony and happiness for all to enjoy. It means returning to love as our default state of living, as the first four letters of evolve imply when inverted.

Over the centuries, humans have created amazing buildings, great cities, social structures, and technological advancements that have given our lives incredible potential. And these wondrous achievements have arisen from the dreams of individuals, then manifested from the hard work of committed and creative collectives. But now it's time to look inwards, and expand our existence on a whole new level. Although life is great for some, it could be enhanced if we could bring joy, happiness, and security to a broader population. The spark that can ignite this flame of transformation lies in the hearts of every leader, and in the words, deeds and actions of anyone who steps forward to drive the changes we need.

At present, we are currently enduring the following types of challenges:

- Global warming, which is arguably causing many ecological disasters.
- Financial pressures under exorbitant levels of debt in many nations and households. The cost of living is rising in many parts of the world because of multiple factors, including government policies, market forces, and our obsession with owning material things.
- Pandemics and diseases, exposing a lack of investment in medical resources.

- Wars, and a huge waste of resources on military forces and hardware. In a peaceful world this would not be necessary.
- Social pressures that continue to wreck many lives, by contributing to divorces, breakdowns in extended families, substance abuse, and homelessness.
- A lack of food and water, particularly in developing nations.
- A distinct rise in the prevalence of mental health issues.
- Inequalities that we can recognise all too well, while denying our own involvement in such.
- A general widening of the wealth gap between the elite and rich on one side, and the middle and working classes on the other.
- An inadequate shift to green forms of energy, which is not being sufficiently well-coordinated across the world.
- A shortage of housing in many countries.

Like it or not, these problems are mostly of our own making, and we are frankly better than that. Blaming others for our plight serves no one and has no tangible purpose. Judgement is the great separator and blocks the transmission of love and possibilities in our world. Every time a decision is made that steps away from the wisdom and truth of inclusiveness, hardship is likely to be the outcome.

Together we are stumbling into a place of increasing pain, where safety, unity, truth, and equality will continue to be the main casualties. Many people are cracking under the strain, and many more will face despair at this rate. Who knows when this pain will call out our names. I have certainly experienced this many times over, and it's been heartbreaking to say the least. On each occasion, my lack of awareness and my acceptance of separation were core causes of the issues I faced.

Unfortunately, we have allowed fear and judgement to take a prominent place in our lives. Fear creates more fear and can stimulate the very dilemmas it rejects. As is often said 'what we resist, will persist', and many of the undesirable outcomes in our personal and collective experiences are things we truly try to resist.

Albert Einstein is regarded as one of the most intelligent people that ever graced this Earth. Early in 1955, the editor of LIFE Magazine William Miller visited Einstein and, during that conversation Einstein talked about the importance of questioning. When we have a problem, it's a problem because we don't know how to solve it yet. We don't know how to solve it yet, because we are approaching it with the same way of thinking that we had when we created the problem. Thus Einstein believed that continuing to evolve our way of thinking was key.

To transcend our current dilemmas, we therefore need new thinking, and that can only come from higher levels of awareness, sparked by new and intelligent questions, unburdened by blame or fear. We need to be led by inspiring and wise leaders who can evolve the paradigms in which we currently live. They need to be open to a fresh way of being leaders, believing in the power of love and truth, for it is within these energies that unity and trust can co-exist as a powerful force.

Of course, we have seen great leaders like this before – Nelson Mandela, Mother Teresa, Mahatma Gandhi, Rosa Parks, Martin Luther King Junior, Maya Angelou, and Malala Yousafzai to name just a few. We have also all seen great leaders at school, in our homes, and elsewhere in our personal lives – leaders full of heart, truth, conviction and compassion. But we need many more leaders of this ilk to take centre stage.

Such leaders don't need to be perfect, as none of us are. They don't need to know everything, for none of us do. They don't need to be devoid of failure, because that is unrealistic. They simply need to be committed to transformation and evolution through the powers of self-awareness and have the courage to step bravely into new paths that present themselves over time.

To be this way, they need to be curious. They need to heal any inner pain that may have shattered their own hearts and kept them in a place of separation from others. They need to move whatever group of souls they lead towards unity and connection, for they will understand its significance. Advanced leaders know that when we weep the tears of the wise, we can't help but heal, together.

It will be a challenge for all who step forward, but they will be inspired by the potential to create new possibilities, from the foundations established by those who have been brave enough to go before them. They will need great courage, but this will flow from their hearts and their power of self-awareness.

Self-awareness will truly be the super-power of our evolved new-age leaders!

## Why Is Self-Awareness So Important For A Leader To Master?

A leader can attain higher awareness by attending university, reading books, learning from other leaders that they admire, researching relevant topics and participating in career-related courses on their business skills, commercial understandings, problem solving abilities and their emotional intelligence capabilities. The list of normal learning opportunities is vast.

There are also a myriad of ways to obtain higher awareness and mental understandings.

However, the true super-power of a leader is related to their self-awareness, not simply their awareness. Conscious leadership has become a new buzzword in business, but it is not really well understood.

Higher conscious awareness comes from deeply knowing yourself. In other words, being in touch with your own inner core beliefs, feelings, validations, fears, passions, strengths, weaknesses and emotional triggers. This type of consciousness can only come from the combination of the intelligences in your heart and the ego-centric mind, for they are fundamentally distinct, but can be harnessed together. The truly self-aware leader has done enough inner work to know what they stand for as a person and what they will not accept.

They are in touch with their hearts, not just their egoic minds. Having deep self-awareness allows a person to lead others in a connected way and from a place of fairness, love and truth.

Historically, leaders have been highly self-motivated and focused on their own personal success and levels of recognition as a priority – the collective well-being has not been their primary concern. Their fear of personal failure has often been high, as this is a common societal trait. In the face of potential failure, they have therefore been unpredictable.

Whereas highly consciously aware leaders can stand for so much more than the unconscious leader. Knowing themselves brings them closer to the purity of love in their own hearts. In this place, they care for more than their own reputation and remuneration. They operate from truth and know that leading from anywhere else is a fallacy. They are committed to their own expansion and learning, but also to the same for those who they lead. They are not obsessed with success and failure, as much as they are on attaining fulfilment for themselves and the people who they lead. They are extremely balanced and see any version of success as more than just something measurable by financial outcomes.

Self-aware leaders are rare in our society, because self-awareness is rare. Our world is led by a myriad of very smart leaders who are incredibly intelligent and highly credentialed – often the best of the best in their chosen fields. However, they are also often highly conditioned by societal norms. They do not comprehend their own personal makeup. As a result, when they are put under-pressure they will invariably revert to type. Their subconscious beliefs, which they do not truly understand, will dictate their responses and actions. They may not even understand why they are reacting as they are. They are slaves to their own egoic sense of importance and fears of not measuring up to the expectations of others.

These types of leaders are not the ones who people will seek to follow, particularly in a crisis. Followers want to feel that their leaders are authentic, caring, trustworthy, in integrity and composed under pressure. They want to know that they can trust the people responsible for leading them forward. They want to know that their leaders can embrace creativity as well as concepts of compliance, and have an inspiring and exciting mindset about the future. If a leader is arrogant and puts themself above those they lead, they will not be fully respected or trusted by their team. People want equality in cultures, not strong levels of hierarchical control where their views are not considered.

If they do not sense these qualities are in place, followers are unlikely to relax and truly enjoy their involvement in the collective. As a result, their potential output is likely to be diminished by the fears that they hold.

Loyalty and respect must be earned and retained through consistently potent leadership. And to be of this character, a leader must know the truth of themselves and have the intuitive abilities to relate to their staff and other stakeholders. They must know the powers that happiness and harmony can bring to their team.

The path to true self-awareness is not something that a leader is likely to be taught in scholastic or career courses, or even in the family home. It can only be attained by truly going inward to your heart to really know yourself. Self-awareness cannot be directly learned in the outside world. It is born out of self-reflection, and by taking responsibility for your own beliefs and feelings.

My book *Where Your Happiness Hides* gives an understanding of how this can rightfully be attained through self-enquiry of one's own feelings and associated beliefs. Whether we are leaders or followers, we all have personal lives to lead and our own personalities to understand. This book can help anyone to commence the journey to discovering their own true selves and start to free themselves from 'group think'.

My book *From Pain to Possibility* charts the path to higher conscious awareness and takes it to a whole new level. However, I would not recommend this book to any reader who is not open to, or wishing to introduce, advanced metaphysical concepts into their learnings. I recommend this book only to those leaders who are already on metaphysical journeys of personal discovery, curious about spiritual concepts and how they relate to consciousness.

Consciousness is not a subject that can be just thought. It is much deeper than that. People in our modern world are looking for more conscious leadership to guide them through life. This takes deep personal enquiry that many leaders, from my experience, are not willing to undertake, for its benefits may not be understood, immediately forthcoming or valued by those above them.

However, if you are open to understanding the real truths of yourself, the opportunities for embracing a fulfilling and potent career are greatly enhanced, for you will be the kind of leader who people are increasingly 'crying out' to be led by.

If you feel drawn to understanding deeper concepts of consciousness, I can assist further; and my other books are also highly instructive on this topic.

The choice is yours, and all choices are valid!

## We Are Where We Are

We are all conditioned to behave and think in certain ways because of the experiences we go through in our lives. Despite this, we continue to judge each other, often harshly, which serves little purpose and adds little value.

Our propensity for judging others harshly (usually so we can feel better about ourselves) has led to a society where many people feel the need to carry shields. With the passing of time, real swords and shields have been replaced by an incessant need to criticise others and protect ourselves from verbal condemnation. Our reputations have replaced our throats as the greatest area of vulnerability to our existence; and our shields have become distorted truths, excuses, and/or denials.

But the fact is: we are where we are. It's therefore a case of how we can now continuously improve, rather than berate ourselves for being in our situation. This requires us to collectively witness where we are, with compassion and an open heart, and to dream of a better world.

That doesn't mean giving up on being truthful about where we stand. It only means learning to see where we are as a society with fascination and curiosity. We need to honestly face our issues and make different choices. It all comes back to choices and decisions! Life is a series of choices after all, and our world is one where every decision has a consequence in line with Newton's third law of physics: every action has an equal and opposite reaction.

If we think we have made bad decisions in the past, there is a simple solution – make better decisions next time! We should not beat ourselves up for what has already taken place. It just is! We can't change it anyway. We need to let stories go, because many can be fairy tales. We can learn from them, then let them dissolve.

This is likely to require a different perspective, a higher level of awareness, and wiser and more evolved leadership, such that those leaders can ensure that our dreams are implemented by the actions and minds of committed and creative teams of individuals.

## Are We Really 'Well Beings'?

It appears that some people have lost the ability to value human life. Yet what matters more than our lives? We are each a life force living a human life.

Have we strayed into a dark place where collective well-being is eclipsed by a focus on personal wealth, not knowing that we need to balance both to be successful as a society? After all, we are all reliant on each other to make this world a success!

Yes, we are too obsessed with importance, and it shows up in our society structurally in hierarchies based on pyramids, and in ever-choking cities and buildings that continue to get taller and taller, so the more elite and important among us can enjoy better views and feel good about themselves.

Here are some questions to consider with respect to our well-being.

- Have we have lost touch with the purity in our hearts, through striving for external validation and importance?
- If so, has this decayed our true potency, and our ability to live simple and happy lives?
- Some corporations and organisations now have more wealth than some countries, and their power to reprice their products to continually enhance their profitability for the benefit of shareholders and executives has become accepted practice. Where power goes, money often flows! But is this right, or what we truly want?
- The average person struggles to get ahead financially, because the cost of things they need and want are constantly rising, as executives in big companies seek rising profits to satisfy markets and their own need for wealth. This position can be incredibly stressful for the masses and their families. But is this right, or what we truly want?
- In this place, the gap between the rich and the poor continuously widens. But logic says this situation could well have a day of reckoning. Let's face it, big companies only make money if people spend theirs on their products, and trust in an organisation can be quickly eroded, once unscrupulous behaviour or attitudes are exposed. If the masses have little money, then who is going to make the big organisations rich? The answer could be no one in the end.
- We think we are getting wealthier as a world. But are we really? Most people are up to their eyeballs in debt, and should the assets that support that debt diminish in value it's quite possible they will lose much of their perceived wealth.
- Are we in a big 'Ponzi' scheme that could well end in tears for

the many who rely on the next generation to pay more for an asset than they did themselves?
- We love our homes and communities, but do we really put in enough effort to enhance those spaces with truth and love, thus leading others to follow and do the same?
- We all know how social media can both connect and separate us – yet are enough of us breaking free of the pack and 'influencing' others towards higher levels of unity and collective love?
- Are all these paradigms truly permanent, or could we change them?

You decide!

## Do We Get the Leaders We Deserve?

Are we blindly following leaders who are not actually able to honour the collectives they serve, because they are too conditioned to think in a limited way? Do they lack wisdom, integrity, and authenticity?

Our future demands leadership that is much more focused on the needs of our collective well-being, rather than minorities with an unfair share of power and/or resources. We all deserve to be led by hierarchies aligned with love and equality, not ones that slap us in the face in order to serve the privileged few.

To some extent, the systems and structures we live within and accept often appear to be manipulated and contorted by leaders who either have control of these systems and structures, or are experts at performing and thriving within them. We cannot put our trust in such leaders. We need to trust our future to those who are self-aware and firmly in-touch with their own truths and our shared desires.

How can anyone know the truth of a situation if they can't even find their own truths and self-convictions? It's not possible! If someone doesn't trust themselves, or understand the power of self-truth, how can they lead people into a place of deep purpose and happiness?

Evolved leaders understand that doing important work is more potent than individuals becoming important. The latter cannot be a person's true purpose. Nor can money alone, for it is just a means to an end, and energy without an honourable destination is unlikely to flow with ease.

Leadership in any form can be a toxic drug for the ego, particularly when it is not challenged, and when it comes with irresistible perks. But all our leaders need to rise from within their expanding hearts, not rise as they strive to inflate their growing egos.

## Leading with More Love and Truth

The antidote to many of our issues is inside the leader, and it comes from presence or heart. Those who do not find their heart will in the future be left behind those who do. It's imperative therefore that we follow leaders who have found their hearts first, not their egos, reputations or wallets.

Looking at it in a positive way, those who do come from the heart can set a new benchmark of success for the rest. This success will come in many forms, but key currencies will be: better fulfilment, trust, joy, and of course more wealth.

The views in this book on leadership and collective cultures may seem harsh to some readers, as it may challenge the very basis of what they define as success. I have compassion for the plight of such readers, for I was one for much of my own career. I knew what I had to do to fit in and succeed, although at times I found it uninspiring and vastly inauthentic. I became a great actor at times; but the truth was in the sub-titles, not in the script for me.

That said, the views in this book are expressed mainly to the maturing reader, to those who are more open-minded, and those who know in their hearts that what they are currently observing and experiencing is unsustainable and undesirable. They sense that there must be more to life, and they can't truly align with the cultures they exist within at present.

It's time we moved into a place of greater autonomy for all, for here lies the empowerment that our hearts desire. You don't have to die to get to heaven – we can create it right here, right now!

The leaders who are destined to take over the mantle and take us to new heights will sense their roles and know that they have much to offer the world, and not just themselves. They will do it because they care, and they want hearts to heal, including their own.

There is a bridge to be built between the conditioned pillars where we stand now on one shore, to the new and more solid pillars on the other shore where a brighter future awaits. This bridge can help move us from our tired expectations to greater harmony and fulfilment for all.

As a race, we can choose to create either through love and truth, or through the energies of fear and insincerity. Things or services created through the latter energies are unlikely to be sustainable or supported by society in the long run, for they are not in alignment with what people really want or demand. We don't naturally desire them.

On the contrary, when we create using the powers of love and truth, we establish the opposite energies through our creation. In this place we bring forth things or circumstances that are more likely to inspire people. This kind of innovation or transformation is likely to be embraced with more positive energy, and prove to be more sustainable and viable; until something more advanced is introduced, which we believe will benefit us even more.

Continuous improvement or expansion is our natural state as we strive for more. But when this more is manifested out of loving intentions, it can make our world an infinity better place. Evolved leaders drive transformation from this place.

## We are at a Pivotal Moment

We are at a pivotal moment in human history, where much of our consumerism, and the economic and social systems and structures we have built, are starting to crack and erode. The sticky tape holding it all together is starting to fray. But it's also an opportunity for us to embrace fascination, hope and compassion. With the right leaders in place, who have the interests of the collective and life in their hearts, we will see shared happiness become common place. Without these new-age leaders, our hopes are likely to just become illusions.

At present, many people have to exit from the normality of life to find happiness, such as by taking breaks and holidays to escape their lives. It seems to them impossible that they might find happiness while still immersed in the soup of normal life. I too lived this lifestyle for many years, until I eventually redesigned my personal and profession lives to be what I wanted, and now every day feels like fun. No more holidays are needed. They are just an unnecessary bonus that I can enjoy if I choose them.

We can all pivot to a happier place, and hopefully this place will not involve fierce competition that only the elite among us can win. We all deserve to do well, and can with the right leaders, with the right mindsets, and with our hearts focussed on a united front. Together we stand, divided we fall!

For this pivot to be successful, we need people who can inspire collectives with their wisdom, leaders who know themselves fully, and are connected to their true self. They will create truth, trust, and real purpose in any collective they lead, like shepherds caring for a flock. Their awareness is their anchor and defining feature.

This advanced leader is not perfect, and never expects perfection of themselves or those in the collective they lead. Many leaders will say they align with this, but lurking in their subconscious beliefs will be an unmistakable need to maintain a positive image at all times. I knew this energy all too well for many years, witnessing it time and again.

Highly evolved leaders, however, will role-model an ability to throw themselves at the waves of change, even if they get it wrong, because therein lies refreshment through which they can expand. These attitudes, if properly applied, *are* perfect!

Such leaders will also seek ongoing improvement with compassion, and without blame or harsh judgement, for they will understand all that's unfolding will lead to bigger and better things, if only we can learn from them. They will be capable of withstanding problems arising from assumptions, for they will know that assumptions are merely judgements, often based on limited truths.

It is truly fascinating to see where we have arrived at as a society, and it's incredibly exciting to see where we will end up if we can apply a bigger dose of harmony and unity to our lives. The pathway from pain and ongoing problems can take a new turn once a higher level of awareness is embraced to take us on a purer and more natural path.

The secret lies in the questions we ask of ourselves and of our leaders, for incisive self-enquiry is the fastest way to cut through to the outcomes that we deserve.

I'm sure Albert Einstein would agree!

**The Privilege of Shining the Light for Others to Follow**

Becoming a leader who aligns with the principles espoused in this book may come with some challenges, because the new-age leader who is natural, who does not follow accepted norms or ways of behaving, must be a trailblazer to some extent, at least for now. However, it's important that these brave ones show the way for others to follow, and I firmly believe others will follow. Like a stone being thrown into a pond, the ripple effect will extend far and wide for all to experience and observe.

Initially, when you start applying the principles in this book, you may feel somewhat different to other leaders in certain cultures or places. But from my experience, embarking on this journey is a great privilege, and will free your soul to express your true self more fully and in integrity. It is highly liberating. And the results will continue to get stronger over time with consistent application of evolved leadership principles, and the outcomes you achieve will most likely make others both envious and curious.

The people you lead will become your staunchest advocates and supporters, and will return the positive respect and care you show them with wonderful levels of productivity, joy and loyalty. They will find themselves in the environment their hearts once craved. It will feel like a home-away-from-home.

Some of the concepts I speak of may seem abstract or theoretical at first, but I promise you they are not. To assist you, I provide some practical advice on how to apply what I recommend in later sections of this book, based on my own personal experiences. These experiences are far from theoretical, for I have lived them.

I also provide some practical guidance and questions to prompt your thinking, which I believe will assist you on your journey into advanced leadership, should you choose to accept this path. Why not be like Maverick and go through that danger zone! Truly, there is greater danger if we don't accept this challenge!

Evolution takes time, but if you embark on this journey with an open mind, you will never regret, for it will help to show you the most important thing in the world with greater clarity: YOU!

## Transformation Will Flow from Truth and Love

The journey of transformation for an individual and a collective are relatively similar in their application. To do it with real or pure impact, one must access the truth within themselves and within the collective truths of the hearts of those in their environment.

Truth can only come from the same place as love, and that's in our inner knowing, or hearts. It can't be learned in a course; it must be felt and embodied. Nothing in life is truly known unless it is felt in our inner core, and unless we embrace it with conviction in our real lives. It must be experienced.

Understanding will take you to incremental growth, but knowing will take you or a collective to a new paradigm or set of previous unseen possibilities. It is magical, and I believe in the power of magic!

Come on this journey into a new sphere of understandings, which will weave together to create new paradigms that your heart may well recognise as the wisdom it has been waiting to receive and embrace. If you see some of the pain I describe so far in your own journey, perhaps this book can help you or your collective to step into a pathway towards new possibilities. You will never know until you give it a go! What have you got to lose, other than perhaps some unhappiness and a lack of awareness, which at present holds many of us back from being what we are fully capable of being?

Greater harmony promises to fill our lives with far greater happiness and fulfilment. But it all starts with the tones and tunes our leaders have the awareness to bring forth.

That resonates with my heart. Let me show you now that this can resonate with yours.

# CHAPTER 1

## Tuning into a More Natural Way of Life

### 1.1: The Code of Happiness Applied to Collectives

A lack of happiness impacts the lives of everyone, particularly the less fortunate. Many of our current ways of living are not worthy of our future together and must change. But how?

In my book *Where Your Happiness Hides*, I considered the happiness of you, the individual, and proposed a Code of Happiness that could be found by taking two key steps:

1. Becoming the unique, authentic individual that you are, or in other words discovering your true self; then,
2. Expressing that real you in a collaborative world with loving intent.

This Code of Happiness can be equally applied to collectives.

For true harmony and happiness to spring forth in any collective of people, individuals must firstly be allowed to be their true selves without judgement, and with respect and fairness being offered to them by those with whom they interact. This can allow them to express themselves in all authenticity.

In many collectives, these respectful mindsets or characteristics sadly do not yet exist, and this causes many people to feel a need to step away from their truth when they interact with others around them. They may even find it too uncomfortable to be involved with the collectives and withdraw from them completely or partially. This is as true in business as it is at home.

Evolved leaders can make all the difference. Within any collective, leaders will all be at different stages of finding their truth and level of awareness. Many will be just conforming and fitting in, to find safety. Others may be full of expression and confidence in their own true selves. It is the latter type of leader who will set the stage for respectful mindsets. This is where steps 1 and 2 above can come into play.

Firstly, when all is said and done, self-awareness is the foundation of step 1. We must know ourselves, as well as how we have come to be ourselves. Over time, disappointments and heartbreaks may tempt us to separate ourselves from others, and deny our true selves; but the more we are aware of this process, the more we can reconnect with our inner truths, and use that to join with others, as well as make those others aware of their own selves. Great leaders know how to manage differing levels of awareness and bring people together on a united journey full of purpose, clarity, and joy.

Unity is thus a great lever to collective happiness, and the grounding for step 2. Unity as expressed in the Code of Happiness can be particularly influenced by leaders, for they ultimately establish the culture that others then either endure or enjoy. They set the tone that others follow.

The more expanded or self-guided an individual is, the more they will then make their own decisions in life and forge their own pathway forward, inspiring others to do the same. My dream is that, one day, the whole world will be able to exist in this same state of awareness and loving expression of truth.

At the moment, however, many people lack both their own inner guidance, and the outer guidance they might receive from a contemporary, evolved leader. We want to trust that all our leaders have the superior wisdom a true leader should ideally possess. But alas we are often sadly disappointed by those who act in leadership roles, plagued as they are with high levels of unhealthy ego and a lack of authenticity, feathering their own nests to the detriment of the collective they attempt to lead. Many leaders are conditioned to act in this way, and know not what they do!

Instead, these selfish leaders promote unhealthy judgements and competition at the expense of collaboration; such that disunity, a lack of truth, inequality and the loss of trust become dominant energies in our homes, social lives, work places and governance institutions. Fear becomes the order of the day and love in short supply. Many leaders will probably be ignorant of the presence of these energies, or not truly care – for they are getting the rewards they need to feel personally validated.

But more is possible in our world. Let's consider two reference points that provide strong analogies:

1. How an orchestra creates wonderful harmonies
2. Nature and the way other beings in nature interact

I draw on both analogies throughout the book to create clarity of concepts for the reader.

## 1.2: Harmonies at Play in A Wonderful Way

A lot of us have had the privilege of hearing the music created by a finely tuned orchestra. It is simply divine, a collective masterpiece that brings joy to those fortunate enough to hear the harmonies created.

These harmonies are created by a group of human beings who are all tuned in together and focussed on a common outcome. The masterpiece flows from the whirlpool of possibilities that is derived from collective intent and individual expression. The love that all the musicians share for the symphony they create is only matched by the passion pouring forth from these highly skilled individuals. Intentions are aligned with a chorus of equality, with each instrument and the skill of each musician of a similar level. There is a deep trust between all participants. The love of music is ever-present. The vibration of the music is a gift to all in attendance. It lights up the chamber for all involved, a deep resonance inspiring and lifting the spirits of the audience.

The conductor of the orchestra, however, is not playing an instrument. Their role is to direct the natural collaboration and coordination of musicians, to enable the beautiful blend of sounds to come together, and to set the platform for everyone to tune into their own unique skill and instrument, so that they are focussed on being the absolute best expression of who they are and what they do. Without the conductor's guidance, the masterpiece is likely to be flawed in some way. They are the presence crystallising the orchestra's shared expertise and energy, blending it into a common representation of beauty, as sound waves intentionally come together to create an ocean of harmony. Their resonance is unmistakable.

The conductor also has their own intelligence and energies to bring to the team. The conductor must be fluid and flexible, ready to adapt and mould her or himself to changing circumstances. Indeed, the conductor is aptly named, for energy must flow through them, like electricity flows into a light bulb, and henceforth brings light to a dark room. In this light sits great possibilities waiting to be fully seen.

The beauty of the symphony is just as much about what is *not* brought to the stage, as it is about what is present and creating the melodies. If the musicians try to outperform each other, or be louder and faster than another, they will undoubtedly upset the harmonies, and the whole collective will fail to achieve what is possible.

Of course, there may be opportunities, allowed by the musical score, for one or a few musicians to play a solo piece that enhances the experience of the collective harmonies. However, at some point, they will move back into the orchestra to resume their part in the harmonic experience or team, thoroughly enraptured or committed to the totality of the sound they can create together, and led by someone who allows a finely tuned balance of synchronicity to take place. This is the formula for harmonic bliss. Everyone does their part, individually and as a part of the unified team.

In this, there is a crucial shift in mindset that needs to be achieved. The musicians must move their individual perspectives away from practicing alone and what might be their individual goals, to what is possible when synchronicity and harmony are expressed through their fullness as a team.

Any collective, organisation, group or team can be like a symphony orchestra, if they are led with the right intent and mindsets. Leadership is so important. It is the cornerstone of success or failure that all can perceive, for the collective team will follow the path that the leader takes.

As for larger collectives, such as businesses or corporations, most have layers of leaders, or conductors, which typically operate inside a pyramid-shaped hierarchy. The possibilities are endless when these layers of leaders are also in harmony and not in unhealthy competition. When the leadership ranks of a collective are fully aligned and engaged for the fulfilment of a collective purpose, they will allow for a greater level of success to be achieved than was ever envisaged (or budgeted for) because in many collectives this will be a whole new experience.

In such places of collaboration, unity, equality and harmony, the result for any collective team will be joy and a sense of achievement, far beyond what could be derived from any reputation, money or title each individual could possibly receive for their involvement. Ironically, in this place where individual financial returns are not the primary purpose, they will most likely end up being greater than was previously hoped for on an individual basis.

Leaders create through their integrity, and how they role-model their thoughts and beliefs. The attitude of the conductor matters.

The simple fact is that: what leaders do, others in the collective will copy, for they see this as the way things need to be done to be successful. Like the conductor in the orchestra, the 'tone' in most collectives comes from the top.

But is it a tone we genuinely want to hear? And, as I mentioned in my Introduction, is there truly a top? The answer is 'no', not in a world of equality.

The analogy of the symphony orchestra at play is akin to the collective structures that exist in our society. If the orchestra represents a collective performing its purpose, the audience is a representation of that collective's stakeholders. In our business world, this would be representative of external parties such as customers, suppliers, regulators, governments, the media and so on. In a government context, this would entail the population that they govern. In a familial or social group's context, this would be the future prosperity and contentment of the family or friend unit as a whole.

Such 'audiences' are invested in the experience created by the orchestra at a concert, having bought a ticket to hear the music. Without the audience to play for, the orchestra has little purpose in functioning. One truly needs the other to thrive. When all is in balance, there is mutual benefit and enjoyment between them. Here lies pleasure, fun and a feeling of shared accomplishment. The money, time and gratitude devoted to the concert by the audience gives the orchestra the resources and joy it needs to keep on practising, performing, and improving. It is a 'win-win' because the energy exchanged between them is equal and fair. Here, love is truly present, for all are loving the symphony and the harmonies that arise.

But what happens when this balance is disturbed and the original reason or intention of establishing the orchestra and staging symphonies gets distorted? And what happens if the equality, balance and flow within the orchestra is disturbed?

Competition within the orchestra will cause a deterioration of the music and its harmonics. It will be obvious to the audience that the musical vibrations are not in full harmony. The orchestra will then have less appeal to the audience, and some may cease to turn up for concerts in the future, or publicly criticise the orchestra, causing its ultimate demise.

This balance is delicately poised around respect. When the orchestra no longer respects the audience, or the audience no longer respects the orchestra, the harmony and fabric of the relationship becomes toxic and polluted, and can breakdown. When one side of the equation is only interested in its own well-being and does not care about the other, the mutual benefit enjoyed by both parties will suffer. The spell of the harmonics will become broken, and trust is diminished.

The consequences of this loss of trust can cascade right down into the individual experiences of each person involved in the relationship, regardless of the role they play in the engagement. Across the spectrum the joy and experience of all involved will be diminished, giving way to disinterest. There will be pain and unhappiness on both sides, be it less joy, gratitude, or financial gain. The balance is lost. A separation of interests will occur, leading to despair as both sides sink into a non-compassionate place where authenticity and true intention is eroded.

Does this tune sound familiar to you? Think broadly about this and outside the bounds of the musical chamber. This metaphor has deep meaning, as this book will explain as your heart reads on. The conductor has such a critical role to play in ensuring that harmony is maintained in the orchestra, and with the audience they serve. They set the tone, without even playing a single note, for they conduct more than a group of musicians. They use their intuition and wisdom so that they can energise the various relationships at play.

The conductor is critical, like a light globe in a dark room. A leader has the power to turn the light on or off with their authentic leadership and balance. The light or the dark is in their hands, and they can choose the outcome that's desired and bring it to life. A bad conductor creates a bad performance, even if they are truly committed and doing their best.

Many leaders today have been conditioned to participant in and prioritise power plays. You might say that powerplay has led us astray! What I hope to show you in this book is that, when harmony and collaboration take centre stage, powerful play can replace any power play.

Great conductors are critical to our future together. We need them on stage now, even if they have much expansion to experience.

## 1.3: Nature Plays One-Song

The word uni-verse means one song. This song is sometimes referred to as 'Ohm'. The sound of Ohm is one some readers will know. It plays loudly in our hearts if we dare listen to its chorus. Monks are known to chant it, and science has allowed us to hear it. The universal song is a humming sound that vibrates at a specific pitch, believed by many to be 432 hertz. It's there for all to hear. Some say it is the sound of light or love. It's actually inside all of us and ready to be heard.

Nature is in harmony. Its song can teach us much, for nature operates from a place of balance and instinct. If it's not in balance, it will rebalance when the forces of energy demand it. Instinct is a natural aptitude where decisions are made and acted upon free of the complexities of the conscious mind. It responds to the environment and natural energies. It just is, and it comes from within, not the conditioned rules or views of others. It is aligned with that one song of the universe. It is an energetic symphony of love that continues to evolve with mystery.

Nature has much to teach us as a collective society. When you sit and observe nature, it operates very differently to human society. Many of its qualities would assist an orchestra to strike up better notes. But here is the catch: humans *are* nature, yet we set ourselves apart from the one big song – and in doing so, we stray from the musical score of love. Instead, we play with fear.

Let me show you more.

## What Can Nature Show Us

When you sit in nature and witness it, it has many lessons to teach us that we have forgotten. I say 'forgotten' for this is our natural state. We *are* it. We *have* conditioned ourselves; to the point that we can no longer hear or see what our inner-sense wants us to recall.

But it's not too late to change and we surely must.

Our 'normal' is no longer 'natural', and I doubt it has been for a long, long time. This applies to individuals and collectives alike, for one is comprised of the other.

Try sitting on a beach and watching the ocean and the shore, and see what you see. Try observing a forest of trees or animals living out their lives, and see what you can learn. It's fascinating!

We tend to walk through and past such magic each and every day without allowing ourselves to feel it. Open, open, open to its deep messages!

## The Ocean Just Is

The ocean can change its colour or outward appearance depending on the energies it is exposed to – the sun, wind, and tides all result in great waters expressing themselves in various ways, each temporarily.

But deep down the ocean does not change. It is immovable. It is sovereign. It is powerful.

The oceans of the world also connect with one another and to the rivers. They are truly one. They sustain life and accept all beings, no matter how they interact with its life-sustaining waters.

The ocean responds to the gravitational pull of the moon. It doesn't question why or resist this. It doesn't ignore gravity because it can't see or touch it. It just is the way it is. Acceptance is all there is.

We might measure the tides on our clocks and watches, but the ocean doesn't care about time. It moves with the rhythm of the universe. Its waves land on the shore in a constant rhythm. They may change in intensity, but they do not stop coming. It hears that one song, and it dances along.

The ocean does not care if you go to the beach to observe it, or even if you like it. It will be there no matter what you do or think about it.

Humankind may influence it with global warming, but it doesn't try to take revenge. It just is.

When you stand on a beach, at the water's edge, you are in a rare place. Here we are exposed to the four physical elements of nature: fire (the sun), water, earth and air. This is one reason humans seek to live near oceans. It offers not only sustenance and recreation, but recreation. The four elements coming together enable us to feel more natural. They remind our minds of our natural ways of being. If we care to listen, they help us to feel alive and free, higher in vibration and connected to that one song. The song is love. Oceans give us energy and allow us to feel free. It's like Spotify on steroids.

## The Forest Just Is

When you observe trees in a forest, there is much to see if you feel into what's present. Trees grow as tall as nature allows. They don't compare themselves to each other, and don't need to be the tallest in the forest. They grow at the speed they need to.

Trees are fully present where they meet the earth. They grow where they are, not where they hope to be!

Trees provide shelter and safety for other animals and insects, but they don't charge rent. They give and take in equal measure. They are influenced by the natural flows around them – the sun and water – but they don't demand the presence of either.

They purify the air that we breathe, but they don't expect a reward for doing so. They simply do it, for it is part of their purpose on this planet. We need them. They don't need us or our chainsaws. Can our egos cope with that?

A tree loses its leaves with the changing seasons. They don't set their alarm clocks for autumn or get upset if their leaves drop off earlier or later than other years. They just accept what arises.

Trees move with the wind, for this allows them to survive the changing weather patterns. If a tree stands too rigid in the wind or a storm, it will break. It needs to be strong, but nature knows that total resistance to the changing conditions is unhelpful.

When a tree dies, or is knocked over for some reason, it does not complain. It accepts its situation and moves on to its next role in the forest. It could create warmth and light in a fire, or rot into the earth to be composted as new soil. Trees don't take revenge if we cut them down, yet human studies have shown that plants are influenced by the moods of people. We often cut them down to make money or add value to a property. I know I did, and I regret it.

Did you know that, on a cloudy day, sunflowers have been observed to turn towards each other to brighten the other's day? If only we did more of the same!

## Animals Just Are

They say that animals live by the law of the jungle. This law doesn't change or take away individual freedoms. It is governed by the universal laws of nature.

Animals go about their lives as their instincts tell them. They don't generally eat what they don't need (although our domesticated animals might, living in *our* world of normality).

Animals make noise when they feel they need to, not for the sake of it. They live with their own kind, but accept the other species around them. They go about their own business, not seeking recognition but just being in the moment. They are alive in presence. They don't regret.

They don't protect themselves all the time, only when they sense danger is present.

And yet they never stop sensing.

Animals adapt to their environment as it changes without complaint. If you have ever seen animals living in the city, like birds, you will know what I mean. They just find the best way to survive, no matter what happens around them. If you chase a bird away it doesn't come back and try and get even. Your family dog doesn't hold a grudge if you leave it alone all day; it simply wags its tail when you get home, because it is in the moment. The past has gone. Perhaps we could try this!

Animals don't observe time, they respond to the energies around them. Nature determines what they do and when. They don't consult with other animals and keep a diary.

Animals just are in the moment, which makes them fully present.

We may see them as less evolved, but in many ways this is a falsehood. They are pure. Are we?

## The River Flows

Rivers are constantly in different states of flow. But as they flow through the various terrains they encounter, they experience different tempos. Sometimes they become powerful rapids. Sometimes they form beautiful waterfalls. Sometimes they flow with great force.

Rivers don't resist these changes. They commit to their full journey to the ocean without question. They are patient on their path.

If rain is in short supply, rivers may stagnate periodically into pools, and temporarily gather moss. But inevitably this stagnation will end with a powerful force of fresh rainwater seeking to find the sea. They always return to flow once refreshed.

Rivers may flood or dry up, depending on what nature calls upon it to do. It becomes what is intended in the moment. It is constantly rebalancing.

Along its journey, rivers not only receive fresh drops of rain, but also the infusion of new tributaries into its form. These give it new energies. It doesn't deny or resist these new forces. It willingly joins forces with them.

The river does not resist gravity, for without gravity it would become a pond and lose its truth. It doesn't cling to the riverbank and refuse to flow on. It lets go, for this is its destiny.

The river doesn't care what humans call it, or where on the map we draw it. It just flows where it is and, despite its important role in sustaining life for others, it just stays true to its potency and path.

The river surrenders to the terrain, and gives and experiences itself from end to end. It is complete in its wholeness and never pretends to be anything more than it truly is. Majestic!

## Bringing Natural Harmonies Together

The secret to nature is its simple complexity. It is comprised of billions of varied species and components all being their true selves, following their instincts or inner-sense, yet it all comes together as one big balanced organism. It all responds to the natural flows of energy.

Yes, some things may temporarily change it, like a volcano erupting or a storm passing through; but in one sense these events are simply the earth maintaining its own balance. Mother Nature must let off steam sometimes, to maintain her sense of balance, particularly when some human beings do their best to make it necessary.

The secret to this natural order is the balancing of one-ness with uniqueness.

Each species on Earth is different to another, although some may be similar in some ways. However, they all co-exist in harmony as nature intends. This doesn't mean one species is not impacted by another, or even lives off another, however survival has its own rhythm and purpose. What must happen does. Entertainment or competition for the sake of self-promotion doesn't come into what takes place. Image protection is irrelevant. Everything happens because it is just intended to happen, nothing more.

One species doesn't try to control another unless survival is involved. Species don't compete because they believe they are the best or want to prove it. We call the lion the king of the jungle, but I'm sure no list of rankings gets distributed among the animals. It just is, for some animals must be more dominant. The lion is unaware of its status, yet is not defined by it, never taking more than what it needs.

Human beings think that we are above nature, and therefore we can be unique and separate to all else. We believe we can exploit nature because we are the Earth's most intelligent and sentient creatures. Stand in front of a mirror and you will see the most dangerous animal on the planet. Being on top of a tree doesn't mean you won't face the same elements as those at the bottom. The wind and rain can still impact on you and, who knows, you might have further to fall.

The way we live now has strayed a long way from what is natural. We experience our lives as normal, but our normal has unfortunately become unnatural.

Reflecting back to our analogy of the orchestra, we have forgotten that we are a part of the one song of nature: the true symphony of life. We have become tone deaf, and we are playing songs that do not resonate with our own hearts. This applies to individual expression, and to our groups and communities.

Nature does not need a musical score to play its song. The song is pure energy and an unseen force, like gravity and the wind.

Our orchestras are confused, and our conductors are oblivious to the fact that they hold in their hands the power to alter the harmonies being played, for the benefit of all. Like a broken record our conductors are directing the same songs, and the audience and musicians are becoming increasingly unhappy with the concert. Yet all who are present know in their hearts that the musical scores could be so much more inspiring, with just a mindset shift. If only the conductor could bring the show to life, like nature in its finest moments, who knows what would be possible.

Picture a beautiful sunset, snow on the alps, or a rainbow after the rains have passed, and feel into what is truly possible when love is present. After a shower or a storm, great aliveness is possible as energetic refreshment abounds.

Nature shows us that to be healthy things must be in flow. As I mentioned above, a river will stagnate if its waters cease to flow, and mould or moss may start to grow upon and within it. The moon moves around the Earth, which moves around the sun. We need to exercise our human bodies for them to be fit. Nothing is static in nature. It evolves as the energies intend. It is constantly changing so that it does not stagnate.

In many ways humanity has ceased to flow as well as it could, because it has become entrenched in its set of limiting beliefs that keep us in our self-imposed cage of conditioning (as discussed later in this book). But like a forest after a storm, our possibilities for regrowth are unlimited. In a place of love, all is truly possible.

## The Wonderful Wisdom of Waves

If you have ever sat and watched waves arriving on the shore at a beach, you will see the power of harmony and flow over individuality and inconsistency.

When a wave finishes its journey to land, it can swish gently up onto the sand or crash against the headland rocks in its way. The rocks are often jagged, abrupt and inconsistent in form, and when they receive the wave's energy, things can be violent, edgy, and dangerous. The path is not gentle or uniform, and the crashing wave then retreats to the sea without harmony being the outcome. It can be a dangerous place to be.

However, if the wave is greeted by a gentle slope ending on a smooth sandy beach, the wave can move across the sand and return to the sea, without that same intensity. The wave has had time to expel its energy, and there is harmony between land and ocean. These energies can meet, and a natural rhythm is established.

A great leader creates a smooth landing place for the energy that arrives from their team and gives it a harmonious environment in which it can be released. They can be like a sandy shore, calm and true.

Many collectives contend with waves of change hitting them, without the harmony they desire. They are like rocks being struck by furious waves because they are tolerating egocentric leadership that promotes self-interest, individuality, and disunity. This self-interest can only erode what is possible on a golden beach of unity.

What is needed is lighthouses, high on the headlands, to expose the rocks so those who traverse the ocean can avoid the dangers below. These lighthouses need to take the form of wise leaders, who can step forth and shine their light on all the hazards that threaten those in transit. This can encourage and support exploration even in choppy waters. They stand for inclusion not exclusion, harmony not just money, and a unified force.

**The Creative Force of Nature**

There are many things we can learn from nature and the way it evolves naturally.

Here are some of the great learnings I have observed in addition to my analogies above:

1. All creatures are unique.
2. Nature's laws are universal, and sensed.
3. All creatures have their place.
4. Nature is constantly in balance, or is rebalancing itself.
5. Creatures adapt or perish; change is constant.
6. Creatures don't own the planet, it holds them.
7. All is pro-created by male and female energies in balance.
8. Instinct decides actions, not information.
9. All move with rhythm and synchronicity.

10. All beings co-exist without judgement.
11. Creatures use what they need, not want.
12. Creatures co-exist without war.
13. Energy matters, not time.

Our beliefs have moved away from many of these basic principles (as covered in both this book and my book *Where Your Happiness Hides*). Yet the natural forces around us have much to teach us. After all, we are created in much the same way as many other animals.

Take the Fibonacci sequence, for example, which is used to derive what is called the golden ratio. So many things in this world are created in line with this ratio. Mathematically that ratio is 1.618, and it appears in the geometry of much of nature. Any given number in the sequence is approximately 1.618 times the previous number of the Fibonacci Sequence (except for 1, the first number), being 1, 1, 2, 3, 5, 8, 13, 21… etc. The Fibonacci Sequence is found, for example, in the shapes of plants and flowers. Spirals or spheres, such as those seen in sunflowers and even seashells, are formed from this naturally occurring ratio. Rabbits breed in accordance with the Fibonacci sequence. Many creations in nature begin as a sphere and grow in alignment with this ratio.

We as humans start off as a sphere – inside a fertilised egg. However, as we have walked upon the Earth, we have gradually strayed away from the golden rules of nature. Put simply, we don't see ourselves in the circle of life with other creatures. We believe our more intelligent and sentient minds divorce us from this important sphere of existence or influence.

In a famous song in the *Lion King* musical, the circle of life is said to move us all from the day we arrive on this planet till we find our place in life. However, our subconscious minds have been trained to believe that we are not truly part of this circle of life, like other creatures. We are above it. Too smart for it! We are not in the circle because we believe we can control it with our minds and motivations. But can we fully determine our fate? Truly the answer is 'no'. Mother Nature has her say!

Our subconscious beliefs may keep us separate from nature, and tell us we are too intelligent to be part of this flow that all other creatures move with; but that is not the truth.

We may dance to our own tune, but it is not a tune that has much harmony at times, particularly when we attempt to dance together. In some places, the dance floor has become a dangerous place to be. In others it is full of grace. We have become closed off and tone deaf from hearing the one-song or universal sound of love. We have forgotten the real steps we once knew in our hearts. We are not singing from the same song sheet as nature. The harmonies we are capable of achieving are out of tune and out of rhythm, and we are dancing to a beat that we often don't even feel inspired by. Some of us are doing the tango, some of us are trying to waltz, and some of us are dancing to the sounds of rock and roll. We are all hearing different tunes.

This book will show you why and how fixing this can come from fresh perspectives and a real desire for positive change. We need to sing from a new song sheet. And these new tunes will ideally come from conductors who understand the pivot we need to make, and who are ready to illuminate this new stage of life with their batons intent on creating collective happiness.

It is fascinating how far we have moved away from the natural world. But the journey back into alignment with nature is completely our choice, and is an exciting one that we can fully embrace with joy in our natural hearts.

It feels like new possibilities are beckoning. One day, they will surely be probabilities.

# CHAPTER 2

## What Tunes are We Choosing to Play?

### Our Collective Happiness is a Choice

In my book *Where Your Happiness Hides*, I explore in depth the power that conditioned beliefs have in determining the lives we lead. The reality is that: we are what we believe, and what we believe is truly a choice.

That book was primarily written to help individuals to see that their happiness is a choice and a habit. It can be found and lost within their own feelings, thoughts, and awareness, which they own and can control through their beliefs. The book set out the pathway to personal transformation, which I can therefore attest to because it worked for me.

This book is more focussed on the collective, and the joy that is possible when a group of individuals share and choose to be happy, and in harmony together. This choice has great power if it is fully embraced by all involved, particularly those leading the collective, for they have the power to ensure that the right tone is resonating for the benefit of all, and that harmony is present when it matters.

This, however, requires high levels of self-awareness and a commitment to expansion before it can be achieved.

The concepts of transformation are similar for both individuals and groups of people. The latter is simply more complex, as a plethora of different beliefs can interact with each other in a group situation. It therefore needs much examination before it can be fully appreciated.

## Our Choice of Operating Systems

To be truly inspired in life, we need to get out of the trap of living only in our egocentric minds – for they carry potentially unreliable and outdated conditioned beliefs, and not always our inner truths. Our minds, through our egos, try to protect us and help us to be successful, which can be very useful of course; however, in the process, they can also make us prone to fear and attached to very specific outcomes in our lives. These outcomes are often limited to what makes us feel safe (rather than afraid), even though this can also limit our potential to achieve and become what is possible, which can then erode our happiness.

Indeed, for as long as our lives remain based on conditioned assumptions and needs, our worried minds will prevail, and lead us away from what might truly make us happy as individuals and collectives.

In *Where Your Happiness Hides*, I set out the two operating systems from which we generally choose to live – from our hearts, or from our minds. Science has proven that each has its own source of intelligence, with our hearts operating from a place of love, linked to our deepest desires.

Our hearts allow us to live from a place of joy, if we listen to them. They do not set limits to what we can achieve because, like the universe, they see the possibility for infinite expansion.

Our minds are wonderful thinking membranes, though they are susceptible to our conscious and subconscious fears, which can often be conditioned by forces outside of ourselves, established from what might once have been legitimate fears, though no longer relevant. Still, those conditioned forces persist.

Another related word for fear is need. Our minds normally express themselves as logical intelligence, though are highly susceptible to the subconscious programming that exists through our experiences. The principle of 'garbage-in garbage-out' plays out here. If our subconscious or conscious beliefs are not true, healthy or in sync, we will be more susceptible to unhealthy patterns of thinking and, in turn, actions.

Our minds contain our egos, which are also capable of distorting reality.

But when our hearts, bodies, and minds are all in sync and being applied together, we enter a place often referred to as wholeness. Here we can know by feeling our heart's desires, and give and receive the love our hearts are capable of, while we can also use the powerful and practical intelligence of our minds to bring this desire into reality.

When we are whole, our egos dissolve into this wholeness like a tablet in water. They do not disappear; they just change shape and merge with our spirit and our bodies in harmony.

Unfortunately these days, our operating systems often interact in reverse to the way they are meant to naturally. We have all become conditioned to think, rather than feel our way through life. We think something, ignoring what our feelings tell us about that thought, then implement what we 'think' is right. Our hearts don't get a say in situations because we do not let them.

Whereas our natural state when deciding, is to feel into a situation, with our hearts and bodies. This is sometimes called our gut feel or intuition.

Our minds *are* great implementers of decisions. They are logical and full of rich information and memories. They enable us to plan, and plans allow us to set expectations and apply a higher degree of certainty to the results we seek.

In my career, I often experienced intense planning in the corporate organisations for which I worked. Strategic plans, operational plans, financial plans, personal plans, project plans and key performance indicators were commonplace in these business environments. As a former accountant I understand the intent of plans, and budgets. They give people clear directions and provide a business with a framework to assess its progress. Plans have an important purpose, meeting the needs of stakeholders.

However, our minds should not oversee major decision-making, particularly for important decisions in our lives, until we become conscious of what is actually taking place in our heads. The filters our minds employ to make decisions are often based on and distorted by our past experiences, although they are most likely well intended.

And plans are not always good. There is much more to performance than just incentivising people to achieve, and plans typically create worry in collectives, because until they are met, people fear the consequences of their under-achievement. In life when we plan to achieve a sole outcome, we are also prone to prevent possibility, because expectations become set and are focused upon. Expectations are the enemy of fulfilment if they are overly prescriptive, because when they are not met, our minds typically create self-criticism and discord both within ourselves and within a collective.

Wonder, on the other hand, as created by our hearts, transmits joy and liberates people from 'plan-mania'. The best inspiration comes when you love what you are doing with all your heart. I ballroom dance, and I know I dance best when I *feel* first and *think* second. My heart inspires my steps and my lead. My mind is just there to assist.

In the same way, creativity often arises in times of fun. I once had the opportunity to see John Cleese, the famous comedian, being interviewed. He said in the interview that most of his best comedy came to him when he was not sitting at his desk, but when he was playing golf or relaxing in some way.

Have you ever had a great idea watching a beautiful sunrise or sunset, or sitting on a mountain top? I certainly have because in these places I am relaxed, and away from pressure and expectation. Here I am centred within my-SELF. Of course, corporate collectives cannot spend their days sitting on a beach, but great leaders can ensure that the energy of joy is available to their team by simply allowing space for contemplation, and fun for enrichment.

You've also probably heard the expression 'once bitten twice shy'. Our minds remember stories of the past – be they 'good' or 'bad' – and do their best to protect us and promote us as we go forward. They identify us as our story, although that story is in fact either all in the past, or mired in an expectation of the future, and just a set of circumstances that may no longer apply. They can keep us trapped in a cage of conditioning that is hard to escape, even though in truth we hold the key to the locks in our own hands.

Sometimes this can be a sensible thing, but often it makes us slaves to the past and fearful of getting out of our comfort zones to take on new and exciting challenges, or entering new relationships. In this stifling place, new and exciting stories can remain untold.

**Our Core Limiting Beliefs**

If you have read *Where Your Happiness Hides*, you will know that I have identified 22 core limiting beliefs that most people have been subconsciously conditioned to adopt. These have been developed with my own evolution as the source. Being subconscious, people are usually not aware of them and how deeply they affect their lives.

I contend that these limiting beliefs impact on individuals and flow into collective dynamics. They diminish our ability to continuously transform within our ever-evolving world, for they install resistance to change. Of course their impact will vary, depending on the awareness levels of the individuals and groups of those involved. And the beliefs of a collective will be diverse, which is why bringing them into alignment for a particular purpose is a great challenge for many leaders. Some beliefs may also be harder than others to shift, such as those attaching to religious doctrines.

Tolerance of this diversity is of course important. But when it matters, an evolved leader may need to galvanise and role-model important beliefs to their collective in order to achieve a certain outcome, because beliefs drive behaviours and actions. This is true even though beliefs often go unnoticed, and like the wind in a storm can be the source of much damage, even though they are invisible.

Indeed, too many collectives try to drive outcomes by creating new rules and expectations around behaviours, rather than considering what beliefs might lie behind them, then try and change those beliefs. After all, changing beliefs is a much harder and complex task to achieve, rather than simply creating a new rule to drive behaviours.

But great self-awareness by any leader can tip the scales in favour of not only success, but true joy.

The 22 core limiting beliefs are summarised in Appendix III for your convenience. I do not propose to go through each of these in detail, since *Where Your Happiness Hides* does this for the interested reader. Suffice to say, that greater harmony and happiness are just a new thought away, and it's the leaders in our midst who can influence this the most, given the positions of power and influence they hold.

Once people allow greater awareness to penetrate their personal lives, they will also feel the desire to see changes in all the collective arrangements they experience. They will want to shift any misalignment, and hear harmony in every aspect of their life – at home, at work, or at play.

However, the power to change the way a symphony sounds, and how an audience applauds, is still primarily in the hands of the conductors, hence the focus of this book. If the audience or musicians themselves don't get what they want, eventually they'll see the merits of changing the conductor. But right now, few participants in the performance appear to be aware enough to see what is possible, or to be inspired by the challenge and benefits of this.

I know in my heart that this is coming, for it is our natural state. Our evolution demands it.

Unless you have heard a masterpiece played by a master like Mendelssohn or Schumann, you will never know what you are missing. I think it's time we all took note!

## We Can All Choose the Tunes We Play

Our beliefs are truly the cornerstone of everything. Our beliefs, particularly our subconscious beliefs, influence how we think every day and how we react to any given situation, even to our own feelings. Our hearts try to tell us what they want us to do and be, but are often left banging on our internal doorways as we ignore them out of habit.

But we hold the keys to open these inner doors and corridors of wisdom.

As mentioned above, collectives, groups, organisations and communities are highly complex organisms, because although there is normally a commonality of conditioning, they can also be a melting pot of differing beliefs and behaviours. They can vary marginally, or in a big way. The bigger the collective, the bigger the pot!

Thus leading a large collective of people is extremely difficult, and I admire those who step forward. Collective bodies of people can create an amazing level of intent, enjoyment, happiness, and fulfilment when they come together as one with a shared vision. This doesn't mean everyone should be the same, in fact this is not ideal, for the absence of fresh ideas and diversity is limiting for any group of individuals. It limits their potential to be successful in their endeavours, however that is defined.

Therefore, leadership is the glue that holds a team of people together and sets them on a pathway forward. This pathway can be well lit, or dark and shrouded in shadows.

When leaders are not authentic and lack integrity, the group of people they lead will undoubtedly fail to achieve their best outcomes, and fail to enjoy their journeys through life together. This, unfortunately, is what many collectives are enduring at present.

But again, here lies such an opportunity for change that we should be celebrating it. With it, we will all be able to embrace a sense of adventure and forgiveness. All we need are evolved leaders who can stop the blame game, and create the harmonies in which love and truth can flourish and create.

First our leaders need to love themselves, and know their own truths; then they will be able to express that to their collectives, and inspire them to discover their own truths and love, fulfil their most productive potential, and create new paradigms of unified living for all to enjoy. The next generation of wise leaders need to know that we need them to step forth and illuminate the pathway for others to follow. No one expects them to be perfect, but we need the radiance and wisdom they can bring forth for all.

Wisdom itself is not linked to age or stage, like experience or understanding. It comes from the heart, which means even the youngest evolved leader can make a difference. Until now, we have seen generations of leaders intent on rising to higher rewards and status. What we really need in this critical time is leaders who can rise from within.

May this book help them to be propelled by the inspiration within their hearts.

## The Truest Tunes Come from Our Hearts

Indeed, no matter what we see or do in life, only our hearts recognise the vibration of truth. All else is out of tune to them.

Our minds, however, only desire the tune that they think will get them noticed and rewarded, with as little risk as possible. In other words, our minds are generally only happy with their version of what is right for them. But do we give them too much authority?

Let's consider a performance by our orchestra. It takes boldness and courage to play a symphony, and it also carries the risk of not being done perfectly. Audiences do not attend concerts to hear a piece of music played out of tune or too loud. They want authenticity and truth in the melodies and pitch, and they will know instantly when harmonies are lost. But sometimes an orchestra, no matter how acclaimed they are, will make a mistake. The musicians and conductor are human beings, and therefore by definition are imperfect. This inherent imperfection is natural and perfect in itself.

But how many conductors will admit to making a mistake, when they could blame a musician? And how many musicians will admit to making a mistake, when they could blame the conductor, one of their fellow musicians, or even their instrument?

Unfortunately, blame has become a default way of playing in many collectives. Our minds are in control, so collectively the heartfelt truth is lost in a sea of mindful self-projection and self-protection.

In my career, I often marvelled at the energy some workers and leaders spent on protecting their reputations above all else. Their work seemed to be secondary, as was the truth. I witnessed many of these people avoid any 'risky' work for fear of making a mistake and exposing their imperfections, which led them to be quite ineffective at times. I'm sure you have met some similar individuals in your own life! Not only can they be hard to lead, but when they are the leader themselves, the collective culture they lead can be highly fearful and toxic in nature.

Have you, the reader, met any of these fearful leaders?

# CHAPTER 3

# Are Leaders Born or Created?

There is an age-old debate about whether leaders, particularly powerful ones, are born or created. I once took part in a debate at a conference on this very topic!

We are all born with an ability to lead on some level, for at our core we are all born with an inner-sense or intuition, and a desire to learn and express. We are all born equal and have a capacity to align with the truth within us. However, some find this easier than others because of their higher relative awareness of self.

We can also be influenced about our ability to lead by our conditioning. Have we been conditioned to believe we can lead others and make a difference to their lives, or to focus on ourselves and ignore any opportunities to step up and lead? Have we been conditioned to believe we should lead where we can, or that we should stay safe being an invisible follower? Have we been conditioned to believe we're even worthy of being a leader? Sure, many don't want to lead in life and that is a personal choice. The fact is, not everyone can lead, because our traditional structures require more followers than leaders. There are, by definition, more musicians than conductors in the orchestra.

But our society and its collectives also have a set of highly developed and conditioned mindsets that restrict and limit individuals, and many of those mindsets are based on deeply unhealthy yet subconscious belief structures. The outcome is a set of behaviours or actions that ultimately retain established and often outdated cultures.

These cultures are also self-perpetuating, since it's often those people who can best adapt to these existing mindsets, and mould themselves to the behaviours they are surrounded by, who go on to become the leaders of that culture. These individuals are not necessarily the smartest, most aware or integrated individuals among us, although this is sometimes possible. It is more likely that they have learned to 'play the game' of life, or business or politics, in the most proficient way, and so are highly intelligent in that respect. In other words, they can best meet the expectations of those around them, who are already in leadership positions. It is typically leaders who choose leaders, and unaware leaders of course recruit unaware leaders, and so the cycle goes on. Unfortunately, these are often the loudest musicians in the orchestra, not those with the greatest desire to be a part of a harmonic group of people and to be of service to that team.

Yet it is the latter individuals who clearly possess the greatest potential to play the most powerful tunes and conduct the greatest orchestras.

Expanding the self-awareness of leaders is therefore an essential way to change the current paradigm.

Not only do we need this change, but we feel it too. Deep down, many of us, including leaders, already know we are acting out of alignment with our own sense of integrity. We feel this misalignment in different ways, but generally it takes the form of inherent unhappiness and/or stress. This unhappiness is often ignored or suppressed by our minds so we can succeed in the normal ways others expect of us. In my case, my unhappiness manifested regularly as pains in my body and a tendency to not fully express my true self. I played the game as well as most. At times I went into my shell and just complied. It was safer but soul-destroying.

Until I saw the game clearly and blew full time.

Many people go to work to make a living because they must. They fit in for their own sense of security, and won't 'rock the boat' because they fear it. They do not understand that their compliance within a culture (which is out of alignment with their own integrity), could be causing them deep unhappiness and an inner sense of personal betrayal. They will instead find themselves living for moments when they can temporarily escape their lives, in the evenings, on weekends or holidays. Can you relate to this?

In many cases, people have simply given up trying to find a way of life that could provide them with a fresh, integrated, and caring culture in which they could truly flourish. Many people believe that 'the grass will be greener' when they simply change their environment – a new home, a new family, a new job – only to be sadly disappointed to learn that the culture they crossed the road to avoid, is prevalent in the new environment too.

This is because leadership patterns and styles are often dictated by the subconscious beliefs most people in our society share, and these beliefs are therefore widespread and hard to avoid. People soon learn that it is best not to keep trying to find the elusive holy grail of a great culture. Some may elect to be independent of collectives instead, and set up on their own to avoid the instability of trying to fit into collectives that don't care about them as individuals. But we are social creatures, designed by nature to exist in collectives, so being completely alone is not the answer. We need others. We should be with others. Maybe not in every aspect of our lives, but at least in some.

It is understandable of course. To use a tennis analogy, most collectives and their leaders serve to win whatever point they are playing, rather than starting a rally that might give them enjoyment and fun. Now, a tennis player with a booming un-returnable serve may be majestic to watch and admire, but if every point in a match ends after one shot, how much fun can it truly be for the players, or for those watching?

But life doesn't need to be a competition; it can be fun for everyone.

Our leaders simply need to take a fresh perspective, including looking into and questioning the conditioned behaviours and thoughts that their predecessors to date have exhibited. As for their own abilities, whether they were conditioned to lead or not, whether they were born with particular talents that suit leadership or not, what's important is whether they desire to lead others with care, integrity, honesty, and authenticity. This comes from knowing who they are and what they stand for, and having the confidence to then express that to others without a shadow of doubt. Self-awareness is step 1; true expression is step 2. Without this, great leadership is not attainable, particularly when times are tough.

So the answer to the age-old question is this… Anyone who has the desire to lead can do so, as long as they are in-touch with the wisdom in their hearts and the logic in their minds. How they got there matters not. Higher self-awareness is the key to unlocking this magical opportunity in an ideal world. So if you aspire to lead, read on and discover how you can truly arise! You owe it to yourself, as well as others.

# CHAPTER 4

# Advanced Leadership Tools to Inspire Possibility

## 4.1: Leadership is Not Management, It's Art

This chapter considers the leadership qualities of a highly evolved or advanced leader. There are many good leaders around, but many lead in a substandard unsupportive way, applying normal conditioned ways of thinking.

There are of course those with already advanced perspectives. I will refer to them in this book as advanced or evolved leaders, primarily because they have higher levels of self-awareness than most.

But what exactly is leadership?

Leadership is a very specialised skill, an art-form in itself, though it is often confused with the concept of management.

Management primarily implies managing tasks so that things that are needed to be done get done. Its primary focus is allocation of resources to achieve outcomes. It is doing-based. It's getting the kids ready for school and out the door. It's organising everyone to meet at a certain time and place. It's allocating Jack to handle the engineering response and Jill to handle the environmental one.

Leadership can incorporate some management tasks, but it's much broader than simply organising others, and embodies more of the following types of activities:

- Inspiring others to go beyond existing paradigms, to experiment and create.
- Creating an inspiring vision and strategy for a team to then follow.
- Creating change, not just responding to it.
- Creating a culture that others can enjoy and are inspired by.
- Creating opportunities for continuous improvement in a collective.
- Creating value, not just accounting for the outcome of activities.
- Creating circles of influence by interacting with a broad network of people.
- Creating growth or expansion on both an individual and collective scale.
- Caring for people, not just outcomes.

In this way, a person can be a leader, without ever having to organise a thing. A person can be a leader, but hold no actual power in a collective. A person can be a leader, and be the youngest and least experienced in a collective. Leadership is a state of being and has, at its core, concepts of creating, caring, and inspiring.

The most sustainable creations in the world are derived from love, not fear. And evolved leaders must do the same.

Unfortunately, despite having good intentions, many people who put up their hand to become specifically named 'leaders' in a collective, fail to then become a good leader, because deep down they are really a manager, or have strong technical backgrounds and achievements – but they are not an actual leader. They assume that good organisational skills are the primary basis of leadership, and that their goal is to achieve certain normal outcomes. Alternatively, some people become leaders for the glory and/or any money that might come with the position. In business, many people want to get to 'the top' so they can make as much money as they can while they're at the top, knowing their position may be temporary, so there is an urgency to their focus on financial benefits. And for as long as they're getting monetary results, business institutions often reward them for this – even though this will likely lead to them and their team being out of balance.

But these kinds of leaders do not understand what it means to lead effectively, and this can contribute to cultures devoid of the qualities people need for happiness and for full creativity to flourish. This is not their fault.

Leadership is an expansive and creative role. Its primary purpose is to create an atmosphere in which everyone in the collective can fulfil their best potential, creating new possibilities and therefore outcomes. In this way, leadership is far less of a doing-role than management, and therefore the qualities that are needed differ significantly. Indeed, leadership flourishes in a state of *not* doing.

So, how do we ensure all our leaders actually understand what true leadership is?

On the one hand, there are many great leadership guides on the bookshop shelves – whether for businesses, families, sporting or social groups – and many such books are of course very good. I read several business leadership books when I was moving through the ranks of my corporate career, and they certainly helped me.

There are also many courses offered to potential leaders to assist them in their role. Large businesses often offer employees corporate leadership workshops. Coaching courses are available to those leading sports groups. Many schools and educators offer parents courses in raising children. School children themselves can undertake leadership workshops.

However, many of these books and courses currently subscribe to paradigms of leadership that actually need to be challenged on a fundamental level. Many of these books and courses focus more on the management of people and specific outcomes. They may use lots of well-known words and phrases to describe superlative leaders, who can act as role models for the younger generation. However, many miss the role of the true self in leadership.

But the past is the past, and the future is the future. New paradigms are needed if we're to step into a better future than the past. None of what I read touched on the potency of valuing life as a priority. Whereas truly great leaders of future collectives must come with the following descriptors:

- Inspiring,
- Authentic,
- Integrated, and
- Self-aware.

All of these awesome words point in the general direction of a leader knowing who they really are, and what they stand for in their heart and soul, rather than what the society around them is telling them to think or do, or how they have learned to behave from a variety of sources in the past. The latter are forms of conditioning that can come together to form the bars of a self-imposed cage.

Awareness, however, can take us into concepts such as beliefs, truths and knowing – not just thinking. It's not learned so much as felt and sensed, because it comes from a leader's inner knowing, not outer direction or ability to follow pre-set rules.

Thus, while potential leaders can and should read books or attend courses on leadership, it's more important that they learn who they are from their universe, for the university of life is incredibly important.

They particularly need to be aware of whether they are doing their chosen job for a deep purpose, because they know that it's where they are meant to serve in their current phase of life, or because of money or to achieve a level of importance or recognition they feel entitled to receiving.

Here lies the difference in wanting to arise or rise as a leader:

- The word 'inspiring' is normally read as being able to encourage or make someone feel like they want to do or achieve something

in particular. But if you look closer at the word and break it down, you will see two key parts: in and spire. They point to being in alignment with the spirit within them.
- Likewise, the world 'authenticity' means to be genuine or real. But what is real and genuine? Leaders must know themselves to be authentic.
- To be integrated normally refers to being connected in some way. But connected to what?
- And to be 'self-aware' means to really know yourself. Again, what does this mean to you? What is the self? To most of us the self is a mystery! Our minds think they are the true self, but sadly they are mistaken!

In this way, all four descriptions require a leader to be connected to who they are on the inside, first and foremost. This means knowing the truth and self-love that is in their hearts, and understanding how their beliefs can assist them to become uniquely themselves, and not necessarily like everyone else. In other words, they have to be true to them! This has little to do with their identity as a person, or any qualifications or curriculum-vitae that they hold. It's to do with them being in the purity of their own hearts and understanding what they believe in, consciously and subconsciously, and how these may be out of alignment. It's about them understanding that they have the ability to create dynamic harmonies, which those around them can enjoy and grow through. It's about them knowing that life is an adventure they do not wish to miss, rather than a competition they must endure in order to acquire things outside of themselves.

Great leaders know that their inner reality will always create the outer reality for them and those they lead.

Inspiring or advanced leaders love themselves, which sits them on a platform of being able to build loving human relationships with others. This kind of evolved leader knows their true self, and knows that others around them are at different stages of discovering theirs.

They do not judge or assume, for an assumption is just a judgement without confirmation.

Integrated, authentic and aware leaders are caring. They embrace fear so they can learn from it or overcome it for the benefit of all. They go through it, not around it. This is a rare skill, for good reason. The absence of fear can only arise when a person is truly inspired by their soul, not by the fragility of their mind.

To have integrity is not a well understood principle. Some see it as just being honest. But the real meaning of having integrity is to know something as true because you feel it in your heart and body, and because you then sense that truth with your mind, and all three are in sync.

To know something deeply is also to be integrated. This is different to knowledge and understanding, which are purely held by the mind and can have foundations in conditioned or learned states. Wisdom comes from integration because it is a part of your whole being. You walk the talk and live in alignment with it. You sense that it makes sense, because you embody what you understand!

I'm not saying that a powerful mind is not important. But IQ (intelligence quota) and EQ (emotional quota) need to be in harmony for integration to have full effect. Authentic leaders serve the common good, but they also know that they matter as much as (though not more than) anyone else. Equality is embedded in their hearts and minds. They are potent and bring light to situations that have been previously murky. Through their clarity and solidarity, they make the path ahead clearer for all to follow. They are a lighthouse keeping all safe as they explore new oceans of expression.

A real leader knows what's important, and they know it's not themselves, but rather the contribution that can be made to the lives of themselves and others.

They stand for potency not importance. They care less about the latter, but stand tall in deep purpose to get important work done. They know that ambition stands in the shadows of purpose for the sake of true power.

Nelson Mandela, Mother Teresa, Mahatma Gandhi, Rosa Parks, Martin Luther King Junior, Maya Angelou, and Malala Yousafzai all knew what they stood for, and nothing could have shaken them from their paths. They were real and in deep purpose, whether you admire what they stood for or not!

Leadership means finding the truth inside ourselves, and trusting it to create a purpose fuelled by inner knowing, and a love for what we do and are. This is evolved or advanced leadership, and it springs forth from wholeness in the soul. This is the self I speak of, not the shadow self that you think you are.

The true self is felt in your heart and your body, and is interpreted by your mind.

Let's explore further what leaders really need to become, for all our sakes.

## 4.2: Aligning Expectations With Outcomes

In many cases, there is a gap between people's expectations of being led, and those who are leading; let's call it an awareness gap. This gap matters, and there is a great upside for any collective that closes it.

In many collectives, the issues that create this gap may not be discussed for fear of repercussions. But people in all walks of life want to be led by authentic leaders. They crave this experience, and some people are fortunate enough to have experienced it.

If you speak to community, political or business leaders, most will no doubt tell you that they are authentic leaders who people can believe in, and that they always have integrity. But is this true?

This book offers observations to help leaders truly close the gap, for the benefit of all, and to take society to a whole new level of cohesion, through greater awareness on both sides of the leadership equation.

Awareness is the key differentiator here. You can only be as good as your awareness allows. If you are not aware that a bus is hurtling towards you, it is very likely to hit you!

As I've said above, many leaders lead with their conditioned minds, and not with their hearts and minds in sync. Those being led can sense the inauthenticity of such leaders, though also feel powerless to change it. To speak up may be 'fatal' in any real or modern day context, so instead followers share their feelings about the inauthenticity they see in their leaders behind closed doors, with those they trust. Such feelings are rarely expressed directly to leaders actually in power, for people fear it will be a waste of energy, and even a risk to their personal security and longevity within the collective.

The sad consequence of this, is that egocentric leaders often then struggle to confront their areas of imperfection, because they see no reason for it. They have already achieved control and power, and no one is suggesting to them that anything needs to change, thus they see no need for a paradigm shift in their leadership approach.

The unhappiness present in some collectives can also be rife, because many leaders use the power of their position for their own self-interest, and not for the benefit of all. Just because a conductor has a baton in their hand and is clearly visible, does not make them more important than anyone else in the orchestra or the audience. They simply have a different role to play and, in many cases, may not be fully aware of their potential to create and inspire.

The magic of the experience at the concert is the combination of the music, musicians, audience, conductor, and the way all present participate to create the experience. The conductor is part of something much bigger than themselves. Yes, they can direct and influence the outcome, but where would they be without the violinists, piano player, or drummer? Frankly, they would have very little to conduct. A baton makes very little noise!

But authentic leadership has been watered down in many arenas of life these days, due to a sea of conditioning that has given many leaders (but not all) a superiority complex. Leadership has in many cases become a form of subtle manipulation. The most tragic of these exists within family units, for they are often hard to escape.

If only those leaders could understand the creative power that they truly have, they could discover a more authentic way to lead, one rich in truth and one capable of bringing forth the power of unity, to create and produce beyond expectation. The sky is the limit for collectives across the board if they were to do so.

When leaders bring their true hearts to a role, and not their egos, and the people they lead sense this, they will add so much more value to their role. Great authentic leaders can generate much greater empowerment and influence when the people they lead recognise them as real and not egotistical controllers.

But it's also not just leaders who can restrict themselves in their roles – all parties can lean towards accepting their position or 'place' and then act accordingly, losing their own truths in the process. It's a form of learned conditioning that can create a spiderweb of unhappiness that everyone gets caught up in. The whole situation can become like a movie scene, with scenes being shot and things happening, but with few people able to be themselves at their core. Many deserve an Oscar for how well they can act at 'fitting in' and following the only script they allow themselves to read.

Have you ever walked through the door of your place of employment, school, home, or even social gathering, and found yourself instantly shifting the way you hold yourself? Your mood, mindset, and sense of happiness can all be impacted as you cross that invisible line separating the real you and the you trying to fit in.

I used to feel it, especially when I went into the office, instantly taking on the work culture's group think, though sometimes I felt it at home too. I went into acting mode, having to become what others expected of me; at least that's what my subconscious mind told me for years. The truth is, when I crossed those thresholds, I became more of the role I thought I had to play, and less of the real me.

This changed greatly as my self-awareness grew and my true self took over. I slowly began to see my experiences and understandings as valuable to record, explore and expand, even if others did not agree with that perspective. This I accept, for everyone is entitled to their own opinion without judgement from me. Still, I began to confront my subconscious beliefs and test my sense of integrity – a test many know in their hearts they struggle with, but would never admit that to others. Indeed, I suspect very few leaders have ever asked themselves core questions such as:

- What do I believe matters as a leader?
- Why do I want to lead others?
- What do I stand for as a leader?
- What are my leadership principles and philosophies?
- What can I improve in my leadership style?
- What would I sacrifice in order to be a great leader?
- Would I risk losing my power or income in order to stand up for what I truly believe in?
- Would I ever put the welfare of my collective above my own if I truly had to?

And even if they did ask themselves these questions, many would likely be incapable of answering from their deepest knowing, for this would require new levels of honestly and self-reflection, and that is not common. It would require feeling not just thinking. It would require inner sense and knowing. It would require integrity of the highest order.

Included in Appendix I is a checklist or set of questions for any reader wanting to go deeper into these types of considerations.

## Tips for Senior Leaders

Unfortunately, many of our larger collectives have become unhappy places, riddled with degrees of inauthenticity, although most would never admit it.

This may seem like a criticism of senior leaders, being leaders of leaders themselves, but believe me, I've been one and I know the subconscious pressures that can be applied to you in leadership. It comes back to our conditioned beliefs playing out en masse. Indeed, when you become a senior leader, you are likely to have spent much time and energy getting into that position, so you don't want to waste the opportunity to make use of your newly gained power and influence. As a result, many senior leaders continue to 'play the game' and conduct music they know their bosses want to hear, even if they think it's out of tune and fails to resonate with their own hearts. They just bury their hearts in a symphony of obligation, rather than breaking new ground and creating new heights of achievement.

By doing this, they believe they will be safe and successful and rewarded accordingly. And many do. However, many also know that playing the power game for personal gain is truly not what their hearts want. It's not their real truth, and it creates a culture that is inauthentic and out of alignment with what they, and those they lead, truly desire.

Set out below is the tune being struck in many larger collectives, as part of the set of mindsets that play out each day in many places. The most common tunes, or traits, of these large collectives are, unfortunately, not consistent with the tunes that most people would prefer to experience and would respond positively to. This includes the leaders themselves.

This table compares these to the tunes that leaders should be playing instead:

| Common Tones at the Top | Advanced Tones at the Top |
| --- | --- |
| Focussed on information | Focussed on transformation |
| Assertive only | Compassionate and assertive |
| Competitive | Collaborative |
| Serious | Fun |
| Needing personal importance | Wanting to lead important work |
| Driven by knowledge | Open to knowing |
| Money-focused | Purpose driven, but knowing money matters |
| Focused on work above all else | Work/life balance matters |
| Hierarchical | Wanting equality |
| Target driven | Looking for out-performance |
| Self-focussed | Caring for the collective well-being |
| Logical | Intuitive and logical |
| Needing to be right | Valuing and admiring the views of others |
| Resistant to change | Understands the need to take risks |
| Intolerant to failures | Able to forgive and move on |
| Outcome focussed | Values learning and growth as well as outcomes, expansion focussed |
| Perfectionistic | Continuous improvement focussed |
| Unaware | Self-aware |
| Time obsessed | Flowing with present energy |
| Thinks to exclude | Desires to include |

I discuss all this in depth below, along with the limitations of some modern senior leaders, giving suggestions for future and current leaders to consider. These are formed as generalisations, and I do not ascribe them to any specific group of people.

Hopefully, the harmonies that our orchestras can play will be beyond our wildest dreams, once our conductors ditch their power plays and wave their batons to create powerful plays, rich in harmony, and a vibration that we all truly know in our hearts, is possible. May authenticity, integrity, inspiration, and awareness truly become the chords and instruments we play to create tunes beyond the expectations of the audiences we are here to serve.

Perhaps you have witnessed these common themes in large collectives of which you have been a part? Do you now see the endless possibilities inherent in an advanced culture, established by an awesome leader for the good of all?

Curious? Then read on and take this journey further!

## 4.3: The Evolving Energy of Our Conductors

Many leaders throughout history have been a disappointment to those being led. Whether we're in a community, business, political or geographic collective, we can all cite examples of leaders who have seemingly let us down.

I say 'seemingly' because to some extent we receive whatever we accept as normal behaviours, consistent with our conditioned societal norms. We are often not surprised by the failures and manipulations we experience from leaders. Our hopes are, therefore, regularly dashed. But why?

The answer lies in our core beliefs – believe it or not! Historically, our world has been most frequently led by straight white mature males with recognised qualifications. They are typically very smart and well educated, or otherwise highly proficient at war and territorial occupation. These males have often risen through the ranks to become rich, or were born rich, because seizing power in government normally takes money. In a modern-day context, these people therefore often come from privileged backgrounds, since well-off people are more likely to have had attended well-recognised schools, colleges and universities, giving them both educational advantages, and well-placed contacts to help get them into power.

We have been drawn to such leaders because, at the core of our conditioning, we believe that life is a big competition, and only the winners get the spoils, because there is not enough to go around. We therefore need leaders who 'must win', because otherwise we too will fail. In more primitive times, this failure meant death, with battles and wars being used as methods of settling scores. Kings and queens were established this way, as were emperors and empresses.

Surely it's no surprise then, that this mindset is still a part of our human psyche – win or face annihilation! Why would we even think to change it when it's so closely connected to whether we live or die?

Of course, times change. And it's time to now realise that this mindset stops the flow of love within leaders themselves, and that collaboration can actually get collectives further than competition.

But the majority of us won't reach this conclusion by ourselves. Why would we when we're constantly rewarded on being well-behaved and not actively challenging the paradigms within which we live? As children, we may even have been told to be 'seen and not heard', and to 'do as we're told'.

In my own upbringing, you were severely castigated at home or at school if you broke the rules and defied authority. Growing up in the 1960s and 1970s, like I did, often involved physical punishment if you stepped out of line at school. It could be brutal at times.

Thankfully this form of violence is no longer tolerated as acceptable behaviour. Children nowadays are more likely punished by reduced access to their phones, iPad, the internet, activities, toys, or friends.

But what hasn't changed is the principles upon which any contemporary punishments are based. Children must still conform without question (often for very good reason!), conditioning them to accept their place in society.

Women have also been conditioned throughout history to stay away from leadership roles, or even any high-profile role within society, including creative and inventive aspects. For example, did you know that Clara Schumann – the wife of Robert Schumann – was one of the most distinguished pianists of her time? She composed a piano concerto at the age of 14 and enjoyed a 61-year concert career. However, she lost confidence in herself in her mid-30s, famously saying:

> "I once believed that I possessed creative talent, but I have given up this idea; a woman must not desire to compose – there has never yet been one able to do it. Should I expect to be the one?"

Similarly, Fanny Mendelssohn – the sister of Felix Mendelssohn – composed more than 460 works in her time, a number of which were originally published under Felix's name. Indeed, many believe that she preceded Felix in the genre of piano 'songs without words'.

As for inventors, it took nearly a century after the death of English mathematician Ada Lovelace before she was recognised as the world's first computer programmer. Her published notes on how the algebraic patterns of Charles Babbage's 'Analytical Engine' could be programmed to compute Bernoulli numbers were ground-breaking for future computer and software developments.

Even in families, it has historically been the man who is the 'head of the household', the apparent 'leader' who makes all the decisions for the family.

In today's society, we are now trying to address these gaps in history, as well as gender gaps that persist into the present, actively dismissing any conditioning that might support the belief that women are too emotional and soft to lead, and are more suited to supportive roles. This is a traditional bias that is softening in many cultures, though of course in other cultures it remains fully entrenched. This bias is of course based on falsehood.

Still, it takes courage to face falsehood; whereas most people want to feel safe and invisible in the centre of the herd – not on the outskirts where we might get hurt, or where our imperfections could be exposed. So we play safe. We fit in. We don't 'rock the boat' or take a chance of being the bravest version of ourselves. We stay hidden. I unknowingly did this for many years, for I was not aware. But then I became aware!

But we need to break free of conditioning that no longer serves us, and it certainly no longer serves us to be led primarily by straight white mature males, unless they are very self-aware. The right person to lead any collective has to be the one most suited to the task, and that's not necessarily the person claiming they're ready and wanting to lead.

Women, for example, are still far less likely than men to apply for senior leadership roles, partially because they know that social conditioning is against them, and because they tend to underestimate themselves as potential leaders, even though they may have many traits better suited to leading. They may also have been bruised by ongoing rejections over the years, and therefore don't bother applying as fervently as they should. We need to help them arise, because with better leaders we will all be better off. In fact, we really do need more leaders who can be in their feminine energies (see below for more on this).

In 2019, LinkedIn published research supporting this reality. With reference to a study by economist Marianne Bertrand from the University of Chicago, they concluded that fewer women applied for leadership roles because:

- Past negative experiences had taught women that to be hired they needed to fulfil more requirements than men.
- Evidence even suggested that women were held to a higher standard than men in the recruitment processes, to offset negative perceptions about hiring female leaders.
- Women were more time-poor than men, due to their higher active participation in domestic duties.
- Women were aware of the masculine culture that was likely to be needed in senior roles.
- Women took job ads more literally than men.

However, the LinkedIn research also showed that, although women applied for less senior roles than men, they were more likely to be hired. This perhaps suggests that women only really applied for leadership roles once they felt sure they were qualified enough for the position.

Sheryl Sandberg supported this assertion in her book called *Lean In* (published in 2013), which documents her detailed discussions with corporate leaders on the subject.

Of course, in recent years we have seen greater numbers of women taking on leadership roles in corporations, helped to some extent by quotas implemented to overcome the many false mind-driven barriers to appointing women to senior positions. However, the balance intended has not gone ahead as quickly as it could have, because our subconscious beliefs are still working against it. There is also still a lingering pay gap between men and women in all but a few western countries, which results from a variety of factors that are well documented.

Our desire to win insists that men are more likely to have the time and assertiveness to get the job done, and achieve the results we need. Inequality is thus well and truly alive in the subconscious selection of leaders. Colour, age, religion, race, sexual persuasion, ability, and so on, also still come into play in our outdated selection of leaders; and even though most acknowledge this, too few of us are doing enough to change it.

I once worked in an organisation where all the senior leaders were assessed for their subconscious bias by external experts. Just about every leader, including me, at the time, had subconscious levels of bias, much to their surprise!

New laws and rules may help; but a unique way of thinking, based on a new set of beliefs, is clearly still needed. Beliefs are more powerful in driving change than laws and money.

## Male and Female Energies

As I mentioned in *Where Your Happiness Hides*, psychologists believe we all carry masculine and feminine energies in different proportions. It has nothing to do with the male and female sexual physicality of a person. That said, cisgender women typically display more of the feminine energies, and cisgender men typically display more of the masculine energies.

Set out below are the key masculine and feminine energies that we all carry to different degrees.

| Common Masculine Energies | Common Feminine Energies |
| --- | --- |
| o Righteous | o Compassionate/caring |
| o Competitive | o Collaborative |
| o Protective | o Nurturing |
| o Goal-orientated | o Empathetic |
| o Factual | o Intuitive |
| o Monotasking | o Multi-tasking |
| o Impatient | o Patient |
| o Assertive | o Forgiving |
| o Bias for action | o Expressive of emotions |
| o Independent | o Understanding of interconnectivity |

Our social conditioning has led to a world where many cisgender men are considered more capable of, and valued, in leadership roles than cisgender women, resulting in an imbalance, not just in the nature of our leaders, but in the culture of the various collectives that they lead.

We have lost our belief in the power of feminine energies, such that we do not readily accept or reward them as much as we do masculine energies. We are obsessed with getting things done, not so much in the well-being of those participating, and we are suffering from the impacts of this imbalance. It limits the role of the heart in our decision-making, and makes compassion in leaders a rarer commodity than it needs to be.

We need to value the whole person we accept as our leaders, complete with both feminine and masculine energies, in whatever degrees those energies present in that individual person. Otherwise that leader will not feel confident to express their whole truthful selves, and will be inauthentic, and destined to disappoint us. They will not be able to foster an environment of truth and love.

Our leaders deserve our compassion and acceptance. They should not have to display only those traits that guarantee them the safest passage in their leadership journey. They should not have to tread well-trodden paths to join others at the top. They should be free to be their true selves, however that manifests, otherwise no one will truly win, particularly them.

### Choosing Our Conductors

In many collectives, it's the previous leader who appoints the new leader as their successor. These leaders typically choose successors who fit the 'mould', who seem to have the requisite skills to perform what the role requires according to past experiences, and who the current leader believes is much like them. Why? It allows the new person to fit into the existing culture that the current leader has already created, and may even validate their own qualities. Since this selection process is filtered through the minds of those making the appointment, their conditioned beliefs are also an important influence, as is to be expected.

But what if the current collective is dysfunctional? What if a new leader is needed because a different style is required, not the same?

Technologies have been introduced into some organisations to provide greater balance to this process, but the technologies do not make the final decision. They are merely an input.

For all the reasons discussed already, as leaders create new leaders beneath them, it is important that new leaders are balanced in their energies and abilities. One approach to this would be to use the male/female energy lens above, to help identify and select leaders who are more balanced.

Any leader will be more effective if they can relate to a broader diversity of people. If they can be assertive and compassionate, intuitive and logical, and so on, then their likelihood of being successful is enhanced.

There is huge upside in a balanced culture for everyone, and many parts of our society would benefit from this taking place more readily. When we choose the best candidates for a leadership role it truly doesn't matter if they are male or female. The important thing is that they have the best available balance of energies, are aware of their true selves and can express that to generate inspiration and unity.

If we can simply apply this lens in all of our collectives, we will naturally move towards a more balanced number of men and women in leadership roles. If we are objective and consistent in how we apply this, we will get better outcomes than the current trend of setting quotas on institutions and organisations to have a minimum number of women on boards or executive teams. Setting quotas may mean we pick candidates just to meet a target and that may not ultimately assist the culture.

When we move to a more balanced selection approach, we will of course see more women chosen because they naturally possess many of the more feminine energies that men either often don't have or don't value. Our conditioning has traditionally led men away from these types of characteristics.

Taking a more balanced approach to selecting our conductors will then inspire more musicians to perform at their best in the orchestra. Balance in the musicians is the secret to improving the orchestra, and the power with which it plays. Harmony is the key.

## 4.4: Why Do We Ignore the Golden Rule?

Most of us know what is commonly called the golden rule:

>'Do unto others as you would have them do unto you.'

Despite its fame, this is a simple principle that many people unfortunately forget. If we applied it more consistently, we would probably have a better society.

There are related principles too:

>'What goes around comes around.'
>and
>'What you put out, you get back.'

Some might call this karma, or the principle of cause and effect, wherein the intent and actions of an individual influence that person's own future.

The reality is that, while the golden rule is a nice and interesting concept, it has broadly been replaced by the rule of self-interest:

>'My needs and desires matter more than anyone else's.'

This principle of self-interest flows into many human actions and mindsets, including economic outcomes, because it is a conditioned belief. Self-interest is primarily a learned state of mind, mostly performed without conscious knowing, adopted because our world has become so competitive. It does not come from the seat of love, our hearts. It's not our natural state, thus more evolved people have transcended it.

Such people, who are also leaders, are focused on the interests of the collective of which they are a part, and their actions derive from a conscious desire to be of service to both oneself and others at the same time.

Imagine our world if self-interest was substantively eliminated. What a world that would be!

## The Three Selfs

There are three core states anyone can be in. They can be: selfish, selfless, or self-centred – which in this case means self-regarding, rather than self-absorbed. There is also a sliding spectrum that connects them together.

Self-interest is aligned with a selfish way of being.

Selflessness is at the opposite end of the spectrum, where you always think about others first and yourself last. If someone is giving to others out of a need for recognition or validation, then that is a self-interested behaviour, although it may at first seem to be the opposite.

To be self-centred is the ideal state.

In this place, you love and care for yourself, but you also carry the energy of care for your fellow human beings that you are interacting with in life. In this place, you recognise that we are all one big family, and you are just as important as anyone else in that family.

Equality in a family or community is important for all to feel happy and fulfilled. When we think it's acceptable to judge and criticise others, or elevate ourselves above them, we are effectively judging ourselves, for the family is truly one organism that ideally cares for each family member. But the same should apply for other collectives, and it would if they existed in an unconditioned natural state.

Nature itself is self-centred. Animals don't spend their time trying to beat each other or devote their lives to helping another species. They stay in their own flow with their own flock, herd or group, and allow all others to just be (unless of course instinct tells them to feed off another). This instinct is focussed on the call of the wild and evolution, and not self-promotion.

## Balancing the Score

For any team to be truly successful, there should be a balance between the entire collective's performance and rewards, and that of the individuals in that collective.

Once the leaders, through their actions or words, create this natural balance, the rest of the collective will feel compelled to follow them, and effectively copy them, if they want to stay in that collective.

On the contrary, if the musicians in an orchestra look up and see their conductor taking all the glory from a performance, they will follow that lead and try to do the same. Once a leader turns a group performance into a competition, guided by self-interest, others will play to the same beat. If a leader wants to keep all the audience applause for themselves, the musicians will also feel that their performance doesn't really matter that much, because they don't get recognition for playing at a high level, and the conductor gets all the praise for their hard work.

Whereas if the conductor sets the culture of the orchestra to be mutually appreciative, others will behave in the same way, for they have been effectively role-modelled that very quality. By the same token, if all the musicians get the praise and the conductor is invisible, there could likely be a lack of appreciation for everyone. The best place to be in is the centre of the spectrum, where all are playing their part, all care for each other, but everyone knows that they are also present for their own purpose and fulfilment. Their own development matters.

Happy people don't compete in an unhealthy way, so when everyone in a collective feels fulfilled and is working in harmony, the whole group will feel the vibration of care and respect and return the energy to everyone else.

Every leader has the power to set off a positive chain reaction. Will their team feel like they are in chains, or free to express their gifts in safety and authenticity? It's like being in a room of mirrors, with the leader's reflection being dominant and there for all to see and copy.

All good leaders must constantly self-reflect as a priority, so that they get the balance right and give others the authentic role model they can follow, so that they are seen and recognised properly for what they bring forth.

In return, they will produce an environment supportive of growth and love. Most individuals want to be in a collective environment where there is joy, love, friendship, and authenticity. Most individuals want to be their true selves, no matter what environment they are in, and at the same time they want the security and safety of being in a united team. An evolved leader can both provide and achieve this.

## 4.5: The Grand Distortion of Money and Profit

### The Concept of Money

Money and drive for financial profit have become key distortions in some aspects of society. It is often said that money is king!

Money is an incredibly intelligent invention, which has allowed humankind to exchange goods and services, and in turn grow wealth for centuries. It constantly changes its form, though the concept of money fundamentally remains the same. Money is also a wonderful thing to have, as it gives us the energy to live our lives, and to acquire and experience what we desire without cumbersome forms of barter. It is an energy that humankind has cleverly harnessed. The concept of money itself is not an issue, and never has been in society. When properly applied, it can enable greater unity and harmony in communities.

However, human perspectives around money have led to unhealthy distortions as to its true meaning and value in our lives. Money has been misused in society for centuries by some. Once a facilitator of exchange and a way of valuing goods and services, we have added to its role that of valuing actual people. Those without it often feel worthless or powerless. Those with it in significant quantities can often feel unnaturally valuable and are revered by the less well-off.

This distortion is promulgated by many of our leaders for their subconscious beliefs align with society's conditioned beliefs on the concept of money, and they generally have the power to exploit it more than the people they lead.

It can be fascinating to examine how this distortion has taken place.

## What Do We Gain from Money?

We all deserve to be happy and to be loved. Of course this can only start with us accessing our own self-love.

In the absence of this knowing, many people seek to fill the hole in their self-esteem with things outside of themselves. There are many things we try to obtain to bolster our sense of self, or our perceived worth, but without a doubt the biggest one is money.

Money can of course bring us great joy through the experiences and opportunities it brings. It can be a great energy in life.

But a whole range of unhealthy behaviours also flow from our persistently unhealthy relationship with money. Many people fight to attract money into their lives, and also it becomes a constant burden. Many people live from pay to pay, and never feel that they can acquire what they genuinely want or need, for those things can only be acquired with money (unless you steal or inherit them). These people have a survival mindset, which is totally understandable. For some without money, they see their situation as their lot. We will call them the 'have nots'.

On the other end of the spectrum, some people have significant levels of income and/or money. Let's call them the 'haves'. People look up and envy these haves, and no doubt many of these richer people enjoy a level of reverence. It validates them. Or at least this is the story that their minds tell them. We can't blame them for this, because it is our conditioned societal belief that prevails in the minds of many.

However, their hearts know the truth. No amount of money will ever provide the love we all seek or make us truly more valuable.

Money is important, but it is not love, and never can be. It's just one energy in the world.

Despite that fact, that money can never fulfil what we think it can, it still creates a never-ending quest for more. More, more and more! Money gives people power, then power brings them more money, until it's an ongoing cycle. Money is seen as the most obvious measurement of whether we are winners or losers.

Of course, there are other measures, such as our sexual conquests, physical looks, or number of Facebook friends; but these pale into insignificance next to our attitude to money. Thus our attitude to money directly influences the degree of happiness that individuals feel in life. Not only that, but this influence becomes magnified at a collective level.

The challenge for authentic leaders here is to set an example, and follow a more natural way to both perceive and balance money, and their sense of fulfilment each day.

It's not a crime to want money, because it is an important form of energy in our lives. But when it is a constant threat to our happiness, then it deserves a re-think!

### Appreciating the Truth about Profits

Organisations, institutions, and individuals typically say they have 'made a profit' once their revenue is greater than their costs and tax expenses over a certain period. I've been personally involved with corporate business long enough now to know that many larger corporate organisations are changing their ways of operating from being 'profit-orientated' to also measuring factors such as customer satisfaction, employee engagement, compliance outcomes, risk and financial profit, to try and move the organisation into a more balanced way of operating. This has been an excellent step forward in the business world for some organisations.

But does this balance exist in enough organisations, or is financial profit still by far the dominant definer of success? Is it the same in families, judging their success by the materialistic items they purchase? The size and appearance of their homes, what car they drive, or where the children go to school?

The answer is of course 'yes'. No matter why a collective exists, even if its purpose is framed and hangs on the wall, if that purpose becomes overshadowed by money, the collective's core reason to exist will become watered-down. All will be forgotten in the dash for cash. When financial profit is the dominant motivation in the activities we undertake in life, fulfilment can get lost in the whole energy exchange as it feels inauthentic and out of alignment with the true purpose of why individuals and the collectives come together. Our hearts feel this misalignment even if our minds aren't capable of thinking it.

Of course there are some collectives that, theoretically, don't exist to make money, like governments and charities. But these organisations are still made up of people conditioned to see themselves as more valuable if they earn more money. So as a result, money can still be top-of-mind even in these types of collectives.

Imagine the outcomes if every collective devoted as much attention and energy to maximising non-profit successes, including the achievement of its stated purpose.

### Who Profits from the Profits?

In September 2020, the Economic Policy Institute in the USA issued a report stating that:

> "The CEO-to-worker pay gap has expanded exponentially over recent decades.
>
> CEO compensation grew 1322% since 1978, while typical worker compensation has risen 18%.

In 2020, CEOs of the top 350 firms in the USA made US$24.2m on average – 351 times more than a typical worker."

In 2021, the US bureau of Labour Statistics also reported that the average income in the USA was US$58,260 per year, or $1,120.00 per week.

At the same time, the minimum wage in the USA, as reported in a Paycor report in July 2021, ranged from US$7.25 to US$14.50 an hour, depending on the state.

The astounding gap in pay rates between CEOs and average staff can be difficult to fathom. These numbers will vary marginally every year, but the story of inequality that they tell does not change, and is not likely to, unless we first change our belief structures. Surely it is time for this discrepancy to be addressed?

## Profit Always Gets the Headlines

Our media focuses heavily on the numbers presented in the annual budgets and reports of major companies, and even governments, as do members of the public. Money so defines all that we do, and are, that we attribute money as the true value of any collective group. Financial profit therefore validates our collectives, just as it does for individuals in their lives; and so the news broadcast carries the 'profit or loss' or share price movement of large corporations. Rarely is there any discussion about the extent to which they have met their purpose or fulfilled staff or customer desires.

What about what steps might have been taken to improve the environment? Corporations must mention this in their financial statements because they must, but do they make the headlines? Not often, unless they reflect bad outcomes or are in industries with high environmental impact, like mining. What about in the home? Do families congratulate themselves on their efforts to recycle, use less energy, or preserve resources? If they don't, they should, as it all costs money and helps the planet, albeit in a small way!

More often than not, however, most collectives continue to assess their success on the basis of financial profits, as they have been conditioned to do by society. The incredible importance these profits carry can then distort the activities of many collectives, and this can negatively influence the way those collectives treat, perceive and value their people.

## ROE or ROEE?

One key success measure of larger collectives is to divide the financial profits achieved by the money, or capital, deployed to achieve it. The higher the 'Return on Equity', or ROE, the more successful a collective is seen to be financially.

But surely there is more to any collective – what makes it tick and brings it success – than just money? People often put their hearts and souls into the collectives they join. They sacrifice their personal lives, opportunities, and time. They are heavily invested in their involvement with each collective, and not just in a financial sense. Look at families, sporting teams, or social groups. We don't join them to make a financial profit. We get fulfilment, we learn, we grow, and our experiences help us live our lives, meet our dreams or new people. We also often get pride from what we contribute to a collective, and from making the lives of others better.

The same can be said of any single-outcome orientated collective activity. Although a collective may plan to achieve a particular outcome – such as raising a set amount of money for charity, winning a sporting league or medal, or travelling to a certain destination – that outcome won't be the only consequence. The collective might also have fun along the way, form new relationships, gain useful experiences for the future, and have stories to tell others once the activity is complete, whether the planned outcome is actually achieved or not.

Think of the damage that a harsh coach can be to the morale of an individual athlete or sporting team, when their sole focus is the single outcome of winning a particular event or match. Yes, some events are crucial rungs on the ladder to achieving; but achieving itself is never the only outcome.

So, instead of just measuring ROE, we could measure ROEE, or Return on Energy Expended. By doing this we could effectively measure the return we receive against the other benefits from operating in collectives. Perhaps it could be defined as:

$$\frac{\text{Profits + Fulfilment + Growth + Fun}}{\text{Financial/Emotional/Time Input by People}}$$

Life is a series of decisions, outcomes, and energies exerted. Isn't it time we measured this more fully and strived to make our perceptions of life experiences more positive? Life gives us substantial opportunities, costs and benefits. Everything has a benefit or drawback. Nothing is ever one-sided. Seeing the world solely in terms of financial profit and single-outcome plans is a very narrow and limiting perspective.

Instead we must find a way to appreciate unmeasurable experiences and possibilities, even if they're more complex to harness and measure than ROE.

At least by discussing it, we can see how a broader consideration of possible returns can be undertaken, and how leaders can be assisted to understand the full suite of achievements possible. From this place they can ensure that their collectives operate from a place of real balance.

### 3Ps: People, Planet and Profit

In 1994, John Elkington developed a model known as the 3P Triple Bottom Line model. This was published in his book *Cannibals with Forks; The Triple Bottom Line of 21st Century Businesses*. The 3Ps in his model stood for: People, Planet and Profit. The model focussed on these three factors as a way of creating financial sustainability. The model doesn't mention purpose, although its overall intent was to support sustainability, which was a big step forward conceptually in corporate responsibility and governance practices.

The shape of Triple Bottom Line business model looks like this:

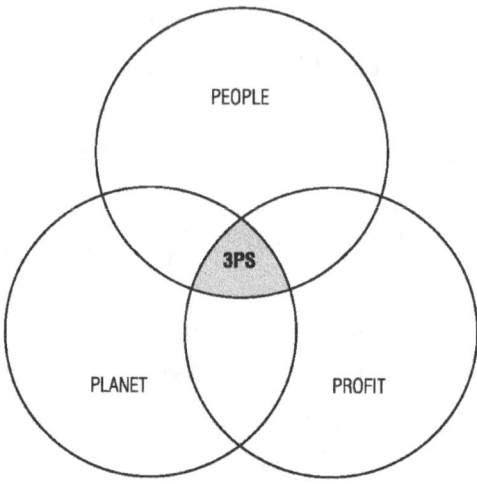

Figure 1: 3Ps: The Intersection of People, Planet and Profit

Each sphere within the business can expand, with the three spheres connected at multiple points. All three connect with fullness in the shaded section of the diagram, for here the 3Ps are totally in unison.

At a macro level, some governments have begun creating legislation and incentives to ensure that companies adopt 3P, and more and more businesses are realising that ultimately investing in this more balanced way will ultimately benefit their company in the long run.

An article in Forbes magazine in December 2019, looked at the uptake of the 3P principles and noted that it had partially been misinterpreted as an accounting and reporting tool, and used by companies to 'show how great they are'. As a result, it basically noted that financial profit had remained 'on centre stage'.

In the article, John Elkington himself said:

"3Ps goal was a system change – pushing towards the transformation of capitalism. It is time to step up."

The article went on to say that:

"There is clearly confusion around the concept of profit. Mostly this is interpreted in the traditional sense, meaning the financial profit a company makes. But this is too limited. The original focus in the 3P model was on measuring societal impact, and thus societal profit or prosperity.

The widespread interpretation of 3P suggests that organisations are doing well if they generate large profits and limit their harm to people and the planet."

Elkington considered that economic or social profit was also related to factors such as the creation of employment, innovation, and the tax paying contributions of companies. Financial profit was needed to keep organisations alive, but should be a means – not the end goal.

Elkington's original intentions in the creation of the Triple Bottom Line concept was "to minimize our negative impacts and maximize our positive impact on the 3Ps." This article (and others) demonstrates the wisdom in the 3P approach in creating sustainability, but the fact is that it has not been adopted in line with its original intent, which is proof that financial profit has continued to be a dominant consideration in our psyche.

Perhaps the concept should be applied more fully now that we have so many people struggling, and so many planetary issues in play? It's already been formulated for us, so the thinking is done. You be the judge! Couldn't a greater emphasis on people, the planet and purpose, along with all kinds of profits, serve us all well?

A more balanced approach to the way we live has the potential to create huge upsides for all. Abundance in all forms is the birthright of everyone, not just the rich and powerful. But we have to start believing in this.

Things can be done so much better, but first we need to redefine and become aware of what we are receiving from money. What do we believe money represents? There are more natural beliefs about money we can consider.

This is a choice for each person and each collective. But if we want to change the paradigm in our societal organisations and interactions, it's the leaders who must set the example, and represent what the collective hearts of their stakeholders truly desire. This will be a big stretch for some collectives and their leaders.

It comes down to considering whether the priorities we think we have, are truly the right priorities!

## 4.6: Shepherds Take the Higher Ground

Let's consider another analogy, that a great leader is akin to a shepherd caring for a flock of sheep.

The flock, to survive and thrive, needs sustainable sources of food and water for nourishment, and safe places to live. Most of the flock will spend most of their time with their heads down focussing on their own needs, typically the essentials they need to survive, like water and food.

It is the role of the shepherd to stay, as often as possible, on higher ground, where they can observe the lay of the land and see what is around. The shepherd is there to ensure that the flock is safe and well, and stays that way. They safeguard the well-being of the flock.

From their higher position, the shepherd can see any risks or dangers that lay ahead for the herd. They can ensure that the herd is always heading for fresh fertile ground, and that they don't stray into a canyon where they could get trapped, be killed, or get lost.

The shepherd must be able to see ahead with foresight, and know what is important to the flock, including themselves.

The shepherd needs insight or intuition to be able to form judgements based on what is visible. Insight and foresight are critical components of any leader, and are best combined.

The role of the shepherd is to care for the flock and, as the name implies, to herd them to safety.

The shepherd is not there to enslave their sheep, but to benefit those who follow the insight and foresight that comes forth from his or her awareness.

Some of the more aware sheep will have their own higher levels of awareness, and may join in on the shepherd's platform of foresight and insight, through their more evolved instincts. The combined power of these abilities can ensure the flock has a clear, safe, and sustainable pathway to take.

Our modern-day shepherds are well advised to hire themSELVES more when key decisions are being made, rather than seek the answers in past experiences, or in the views of expensive consultants.

The intuition that we all carry within our higher selves is free to use, and is always

available. It's our real centre of knowing, and our insightful teacher within. All our shepherds need to do is give it important jobs and trust it's responses. It never lets you down.

So our leaders are meant to be like shepherds, creating sustainable resources, shining a light on the best pathway forward for those prepared to follow the collective path. Two-way trust, respect and care are needed for the shepherd to lead a successful herd forward.

However, the allure of higher ground often attracts leaders to the role for the wrong reasons. Let's explore this further.

### The Allure of Higher Ground

Leadership has arguably become distorted in our society by our conditioned beliefs around status. Just the title 'leader' can make some people want to lead, regardless of their individual aptitude or experience. They want it because they believe it will give them status and more money. They want to be more important than others. They see the leader currently elevated in their higher position, possibly even in higher physical location, such as a castle on a hill, and want to be elevated above others as well.

But no leader is more important than the collective they lead. Leadership is simply a role within that team, driven by the capability to connect with and influence others. Indeed, human success and fulfilment must be based on equality as a core concept, because importance and superiority are detrimental concepts that bring us all down. Certainly we can all aspire to undertake or lead important work. But the moment we seek or think we have personal importance above others, the game is up.

Those leaders who think they are more important than anyone helping the team to fulfil the collective's important purpose, are limiting that collective's latent potential.

There is a big difference between stature and status. The former implies height, the latter implies importance.

### The Limited Pathways of Today

Many modern-day leaders today, because of their conditioning, do not act as shepherds, but as controllers. Unfortunately, there is no love in control, not like there is in freedom and trust.

Most leaders create narrow pathways through which only they can reach higher states of abundance or well-being. They don't guide their flocks to better places where there is shared well-being, consciousness, happiness, and abundance. They misunderstand their role, driving the flock to primarily make their life easier.

I once had the experience of being told, upon promotion to a higher role, that my service to the business I worked for should now be the number one priority in my life, above family, even my own life. I was shocked by this. The well-being of the people in any collective should matter greatly, for they are the ones that are life living life. It must, however, be properly balanced with the collective well-being.

When you put a person's career in context, that person is working in a role to support their own lifestyle and meet their own needs first and foremost. When a leader fails to recognise that a worker's career is primarily for the happiness of the worker, not the organisation they are employed by, the employee senses this lack of integrity, and they hold parts of themselves back from the team. This is not likely to be expressed openly, but it is always energetically present, and can be felt by those who are observant in the team.

Some sheep are also often herded by wolves in sheep's clothes. Many sheep that sense this inauthenticity, however, still follow the chosen path in a state of fear and distrust. They are not sure what other paths are available for them to take, other than to join another flock if it accepts them.

The herd therefore adopts the existing mentality of self-interest and control, and many of them in the herd then also aspire to be in control. They focus on surviving, though dream of thriving. They want to sit on the hill and be in charge.

Who wouldn't, right? When the leader earns 'big bucks' and gets to sit in a lofty place with most of the perks, is it any wonder that many members of collectives also want to be in charge and sit on the higher ground? It's understandable, isn't it?

But collective well-being must also sit at the forefront of our society, and leaders are the ones who need to lead by example, for others to follow. If they instead set narrow pathways for their followers to follow, they limit us all.

### The Fake Pedestal

Many of us have sensed or witnessed leaders not being completely open about the truth. They may even elect to deny the truth if it's contrary to the image they want to project or protect. I witnessed it many times in business, we see it often in politics, and family leaders often do this too. We have become a society where we hate being wrong or seen to fail.

Our minds tell us that, to be able to lead, leaders must be right and superior to others. This is a conditioned mindset we have inherited from the past. Good leaders must be serious, in control and right. We put them on a pedestal, and they believe that this pedestal brings them higher powers and intelligence, which demands to be honoured and treated with reverence.

On this pedestal, however, fear steps in to greet them. What if the pedestal collapses? What if I fall off? What if people see the real me and I must step down from my role?

Control, seriousness, and righteousness find their way onto that pedestal. Fun steps down. Their ego demands that the leader stay on the pedestal, or even step onto a higher one. After all, aren't they superior and entitled to the position they've achieved.

A great analogy is the story of the *Wizard of Oz*. The wizard is thought to be all powerful and superior. He projects this image to the outside world, never revealing his true self until the end of the story, when he is finally exposed as just a normal person, with no magical powers, just money, a castle on the hill and a mega-phone.

We have allowed our world to become full of fake wizards, and there are many people only too prepared to live in the castle, and project control and superiority for their own purpose, led by fear. But we need more Dorothy's who are prepared to step up and challenge the fantasy!

## The Naked Truth

General George Patton, the American World War II General, said that he went to the front line to visit his troops, just so they could see that he was a man just like them, and imperfect. He noted that, in their hearts, people truly want to be led by people who are not perfect. This makes them authentically human and believable.

But how many leaders, whether political, business, community or family leaders, ever step up to the microphone and admit they could have done better? Some, but not many! If they do, their ego will certainly look to find something or someone outside of themselves to blame for the failure. Their tune is always upbeat, and the melody wonderful.

Perfectionism has long been an issue I have had to contend with myself, both in my personal life and my career. But the trouble with perfectionism is that it stifles creativity and learning. People are less likely to express their views, take on a new project or apply for a new job, for instance, if they fear not measuring up to the expectations of their own minds, or the minds of their colleagues or other leaders. In my experience of collectives, this tends to shut down honesty and integrity. Why tell the truth about an error if you can cover it up or blame it on someone else? Why even step forward to take on a difficult challenge if your collective is likely to ostracise or punish you for being imperfect? The fact is that only those with great courage would do so willingly.

Courageous leaders, however, try to turn mistakes into learning opportunities. Of course, a mistake made too many times, despite clear feedback, may require more drastic action, such as assisting those involved to find more suitable roles.

When I was a leader, I always tried to be extremely open about personal issues I was dealing with, such as my divorces. This vulnerability helped me to be seen as authentic and real. No matter what level we reach, we are all human with feelings and issues. To hide them too much is to step away from our truth.

Warren Buffet, the well-known investor, is famous for saying that "when the tide goes out, you get to see who has been swimming naked." The truth, in other words, often gets exposed as circumstances change, so why not embrace the naked truth from the very beginning?

Unfortunately, we have become used to being fed half-truths, and when the full truth is eventually exposed, the conductor responsible may be well and truly gone, having left others to pick up the pieces. We then easily accept a new leader, but with increasing levels of distrust, which becomes 'like water off a duck's back'. Our minds perversely seek perfection, yet are happy to accept something less of others if there are no or low consequences for ourselves. It's all out of tune and back to front, like a musical score written by a drunk.

Perfectionism is ultimately the enemy of authenticity and truth, for it demands that people become something that is never possible for them to be – perfect.

Part of the problem is of course image. We have strayed a long way from the famous saying that: what you think of me is none of my business. In fact, these days we make it our business to manage our image in many areas of life, rather than just being our authentic truth.

Do you have an image point? How much energy do you put into maintaining and inflating it? Most of us do unknowingly. I know I did for most of my life. And it's not that we ever really lose our image, it's more a question of how much we buy into it. Does it validate us, or does it just help us into a position that will help us follow our chosen path?

Whatever the reason, our continuous focus on image and perfectionism can only lead to the distortion of truth. We need to be more naked, because it's authenticity that truly connects people, not a perfect image no one can believe.

## 4.7: Embracing the Energy of Fear

Some leaders are prone to make short-term self-interested decisions based on personal fear at the expense of the collective well-being. This appears to be particularly so in politics, where re-election is required every few years. This approach is very normal.

The propensity to need to be seen as strong and perfect is typical of many modern leaders, but unfortunately all this serves to do is to mask the deep vulnerability and fear that stops them from being truly present and aligned with their greatest intelligence that naturally resides inside them. They hide behind bravado, excuses, self-promotion, self-protection and, sometimes, aggression. They don't realise that this only tells everyone around them that they're afraid. Aggressive bullies in the playground always have the greatest fears.

Yet imagine a world where leadership came without self-promotion or self-interest getting in the way of the truth. Imagine if leaders were recognised for saying it 'as it is', and we rewarded our messengers and didn't shoot them just because the truth they raised was inconvenient, or required money or work to fix the problems being exposed. This would be a more natural way for us all to live. It would also give our leaders a more natural platform to lead from, not a shaky pedestal they weren't sure they could trust and would collapse in a storm.

I was an auditor for much of my career, and I know only too well the resistance that leaders can bring to inconvenient truths. Transcending fear is one of the great differentiators between good and bad leaders. But this requires respecting fear itself, not hiding from it. We must face it front on then transcend it with truth and vulnerability.

Feelings that arise from fear can in fact be our doorway to greater awareness.

As Mark Twain famously said,

"Face your fear and the death of fear is certain."

The negativity you express when afraid can also often heighten the chances of bringing that very event or thing forward into your circumstances. So of course we should put in place appropriate risk management steps to limit the damage from any potentially negative event; but we should equally avoid spending our lives worrying about or obsessing over fear, as this leaves little room for excitement and positivity to descend into your experiences. This also applies to collectives on a magnified scale.

When we wonder about a circumstance, and avoid worry, fear can play a lesser role.

## Our Obsession with Conquering Fear

Fear can be a destructive force in our lives. It can also be an ally.

Those able to stand in a place of true leadership know themselves to be fearless, not because they have conquered fear, but because they have learned to understand it as an important indicator they can harness. It becomes an ally in the war with themselves.

When a true leader understands the fear that arises either within themselves or in the people they lead, they can see through it. They feel and know its presence deeply within themselves, and they do not waste their energy trying to conquer it.

To try and conquer it comes from a place of egocentric achievement, which is itself another fear. When we fall into a state of fear and let it overwhelm us, it becomes a weapon, and we commonly direct that weapon at both ourselves and others. This is often highly destructive, and in the case of a leader, makes it harder for them to make sound and effective decisions for the benefit of all. Love conquers all, including fear – if we surrender to it!

As mentioned above, it is important for a leader to lead from a place of inspiration, for here in their hearts lies their purity of purpose. When a leader notices that there is an energy of fear, or confusion, within themselves or their people, a true leader will therefore immerse him or herself in the knowledge that they will transcend their fear, that it is a temporary state, and that they may even be able to guide others from this powerful state.

Confusion always precedes clarity. So we should also embrace confusion when it arises, because we can love the possibilities it brings forth.

Accepting fear and confusion takes great courage of course. To transcend the fear within themselves or others, a truly evolved leader must be willing to face it and explore it, which requires the ability to access and sense into their authentic feelings. But is it possible for all of us to do this?

Most of the Earth was opened up by brave explorers, who had the curiosity to accept their fears, and go into uncharted waters and lands. From this place new possibilities were established, new civilisations were founded, and new resources were discovered. Great possibilities await us too, if we can find the wisdom to honour our fears and confusion, and in turn to step into a place of inspiration and boldness.

Boldness is found in the absence of fear. This is far more powerful than its cousin, courage, which implies someone is taking steps with fear in their 'hearts'. Recognition and transcendence of fear is always the beginning of great consciousness and opportunity, which we are all capable of achieving and which many among us are ready to pursue. All we have to do is realise that facing fear is a great doorway to freedom. We can't run from it and be successful.

Our hearts, it has been proven, have a great intellect, distinct from that we hold and express through our minds. This is because it is linked to our true essence or intuition, and from here we can inspire ourselves and others. This connection is sometimes called 'presence'. Presence is available to everyone who wishes to hear what it has to say. We simply need to listen with our intuition and sense into its clarity.

The leader who has this wisdom – exploring the fear within themselves, and transcending it by feeling into its wisdom – can reach a place of great intelligence and balance. This means understanding that a fear is an indicator that we can connect to and learn from. To transcend means to go through something, then go beyond it. It is possible to do this with any fear. In this place great leaders are highly conscious and in their full power. This is not a power we have traditionally associated with most leaders. Many of the traits we have mistakenly admired in leaders are actually weaknesses, for they mask unexpressed anxieties baked in the oven of fear. Fear can take a leader to a hostile place where conflict resides.

But highly evolved leaders can lead others with consummate ease through uncertainty, for in this energy they are not seeking certainty or recognition, but are fresh in the perspective that comes from being able to explore possibility and ambiguity.

The albatross is a curious sea bird. It lives at sea, and rarely comes to shore, unless it seeks to breed. The albatross is capable of living without the certainty of a reference point. It is instinctively comfortable in a place of adventure, and the unknown. The albatross can move with great speed, and grace and is a welcome sight for sailors on a journey of the unpredictable seas. Great leaders can be like the albatross. They can inspire others with their lack of fear, and their willingness to live without the reference points we might call normality. They will soar into the blue sky and sustain themselves without the certainty that a safe harbour could provide.

Our hearts can embrace ambiguity, like the albatross embraces its natural gifts. Our hearts are our greatest teachers, and can lead us into presence and possibility from within. Our minds, left alone, cannot do this for they are immersed in story and memory, not the powerful knowing found in the presence of life. Aware leaders can take us all on a wonderful journey of evolution, once they transform themselves. Step by step they can shine a light on what has been hiding in the shadows of our possibility. They can conduct the natural harmonies that can spring forth, from valuing the journey to being more, not just wanting to consume and own more.

Our need for certainty is also a form of expectation, which is the enemy of possibility and fun. It is a common human condition to yearn for certainty, for it is linked to our underlying subconscious fear of death and/or irrelevance. Yet, since life rarely follows the script we write, or respects our desire to be its director, the need for certainty will inevitability invite disappointment into our lives. To believe that we might be able to know or predict the future is a complete falsity, and every great leader knows that and stands ready to respond to what life presents, not only what was hoped for. Hope springs eternal, but it can also prove to be an illusion of the mind.

The boldest leaders revel in this energy, for they take on the challenge of ambiguity, and confront their own strengths and fearlessness. The most powerful leaders know that to expand they need to be open to the discomfort that fear can bring forth. Fear is a great and powerful teacher that they respect. But this triumph requires the ability to feel and, despite the exhilaration and colour emotions can provide to our lives, many leaders today, or individuals for that matter, have lost their ability or willingness to access their feelings, and to then confront them.

Emotions are truly a privilege we share as humans and should be honoured. Ignoring these vital messages from our bodies is a fast track to living without active intuition. I lived this way for part of my early career, until I learned the benefits of being vulnerable and feeling my way through life.

### The Power of Peace

Peace in our world can be hard to find because we have come to see peace as being aligned with weakness.

Many leaders throughout history have been warriors, and warriors are not supposed to take a backward step. They must win, control, and compete. It's them against the world! How many wars have been fought and lives destroyed or lost throughout the centuries because such leaders, normally men, let their egos get the better of them, and so they decide to wage war? Why have we given them this insane level of power over our lives, when they are more like children in the playground fighting over toys?

War is the saddest, most pathetic side effect of human insecurity and lack of self-love, and truly should never occur. It's a sad litany of despair and unhappiness. We have reached an unacceptable place when we think that taking human lives is the only way to settle a dispute!

When any person is aggressive towards another, it is often just a reflection of their own inner turmoil or conditioning. When such a person then attempts to lead others with hate, it equates to lazy leadership – merely manipulating the ever-present energy of fear that lurks in the minds of others, who may have not yet learned to access the peace in their own hearts. It is easy to inspire hate, and encourage humans to cause each other great pain, just by sparking the fear that already lurks inside their conscious and subconscious minds. Such leaders have truly failed in the quest to be true leaders, and create happy collectives. How long will it take us to learn this lesson? We have celebrated too many leaders throughout history who have conquered other tribes or nations. It is a badge of honour that needs to be melted down and scrapped forever-more. It is time we changed our perception of peace. It is never the outcome of weakness, for conflict is the real representation of weakness.

Sophisticated leaders always seek to create peace out of any situation. This doesn't mean that they roll-over and give in to a party seeking to deny them their rights, to take away their resources or autonomy. To do so smacks of a lack of self-respect. There are times when we must defend ourselves. Leaders of family units must have enough respect for themselves that they stand true to their resolve. Leaders of community groups must respect their collective's purpose enough to campaign for its continued resources, if not existence. Leaders of geographical regions need to respect boundaries to protect people.

But true leaders must also be able to transcend differing views, and offer love to those experiencing pain. An evolved leader understands this, and that it takes great strength and extraordinary leadership to create peace, while at the same time making decisions in the best interests of the collective. Differences are truly unavoidable in life and in groups of people, so why even fight it?

Let's not forget that we all share this world and fundamentally we are all the same. Having control or power over others is thus a fallacy, for we are all one and all equal. There is no love in control, and true power can only come from love. Since we are all one, when you judge another you are effectively judging yourself. This is the very essence of Karma. Happy people and countries do not start wars and don't need to have power over one another. Hurt people hurt others. Healed people heal others!

In the frame of mind of compromise and unity, anything is possible.

That said, it is important to have compassion for leaders who have as yet been unable to strike up the chords of harmony, for their own awareness has most likely not allowed it. They are the product of thousands of years of human obsession with winning over others. Their conditioning has very deep roots throughout history.

But at our core, we are pure love and love can be one-directional. We can love those who dislike us, and in the process bring forth greater harmonies, for let's not forget that every action has an equal and opposite reaction. The wise leader leads and lives from this perspective, and knows that wise leadership can only emanate from the heart.

Change the beliefs, and the leaders we really need will bring true prosperity into our lives. It's coming. I feel it. Then I think it!

### Appreciating the Views of Others

The masculine energy of righteousness is a dangerous energy for a leader to have. Righteousness is not simply having confidence or surety, but is an overwhelming belief in being right that allows a leader to think they 'know it all'. It's common for such people to want to be seen as superior and, more than likely, perfect. Righteousness lacks care for others. I'm right, you're wrong, and I don't care what you think, I'm going to ignore you and get what I want.

Righteousness blocks the spreading of new ideas, and it is the enemy of listening. How many leaders don't truly listen, for their thirst for importance tells them that their view is the only one that matters.

Early on in my career, I know I didn't listen as closely as I should have to the views of others. I formed my own views, and didn't see how my awareness could be enhanced by the views of others. It was a very masculine mindset that I have let go of in later life.

In fact, a true leader cares less about failing or being unpopular. They prefer neither, but they don't fear either. They simply stand for the well-being of all, and in this energy they are open to fresh ideas, for they know that they are not the fountain of all wisdom. They also know that if a leader sees a problem through the lens of stress, it can't help but feed through to the entire group who are interacting together, and produce stress on multiple fronts.

A true leader is an advocate of transformation, and magnificent transformation requires unity, which comes from a leader inviting the views of all to come forth.

Such a leader wants to hit the right note, and has no need to be 'big-noted'. Adopting the views of others and carrying forward all the great ideas that arise from within the 'team' is not weak. It represents integrity and respect for the intelligence of others, as long as the leader recognises the true source of that wisdom.

We are all truly equal, and no one person has a monopoly on great ideas – not even the highest-ranking leader in all the world. How could they, when they have only lived their one and only life, and only experienced their own experiences? How could they when they have developed into the person they have from only one set of events, in a certain number of places, surrounded by a certain number and type of people? It is impossible for any one person to have insight into everything.

Compassion for the truths of all is the key. I admit that it took me a number of years to truly come to terms with this principle and to embody it.

Age and experience are also not prerequisites for wisdom. It is those who have just entered an environment, such as the young or newly arrived, who often have fresh ideas and may see how collective norms might be holding people back from reaching their true potential.

We are each intelligent in our own way. We are all different and have much to add to a situation.

Thus one of the most powerful attributes of a truly evolved leader is their ability to stand in admiration of the views of others, even if they disagree wholeheartedly with those views. This energy is rare, for most of us fear rejection and being belittled by others. We need to win, as in the absence of victory we often feel deflated.

A leader who can transcend this fear, to the point that they can express admiration for those they disagree with, can often then disarm aggressive advocates for contrary views, bewildering them because they don't know how to respond to this energy of love and compassion. But if you try this with others, you will see and feel its potency. When somebody listens to your views with compassion and understanding and respects them, despite not adopting them, how do you feel? Feeling accepted and listened to are most likely your initial responses, and in this energy of respect, true compromise and understanding for all is possible.

More compassion and less aggression, more listening and less talking, and a greater presence is all necessary to reach this highly evolved level of leadership. A sophisticated leader embraces all and brings love and intelligence to all situations. Such leaders are open to all perspectives and possibilities. They broaden the possibility of responses that can be applied to any circumstance, particularly in a crisis that they may not have faced before, therefore leading their collectives into safety, where they can thrive.

### The Monetisation of Fear

For centuries, governments and religious collectives have used fear to sell products and services. They manipulate others into believing that they desire or need certain things to be complete and to fit in. Fear has now become so prominent in our world, that it is used as a daily weapon to make money and to gain power over others.

But when someone fears that they are incomplete without a certain thing in their lives, they open themselves up to a mild form of slavery, and manipulation. They become the slaves of fear.

In truth, these restraints and restrictions are self-imposed by the imposter within our minds, which tells us we are in need. Many of us feel incomplete without this mild slavery we embrace so readily. The reality is that this type of slavery is often maintained and policed by the slaves themselves. The slaves have the keys to their own freedom, but they simply don't know where they lost them, or that they ever had them.

Of course, history has experienced ugly versions of physical slavery, like that experienced in Northern America before the Civil War in the 1860s. But the slavery we see today is more akin to a loss of our own autonomy, in the face of economic pressures or our fear of failure.

Most of us in advanced countries have the good fortune these days to be able to choose our own lives, and all that we do and become. But we also can't seem to appreciate the freedom of this with ease. We choose obligation and commitment over fun and joy, and in doing so create stress and unease.

It took me over 50 years to find this awareness myself, that happiness is a choice and a habit. Then finally one day I awoke to the fact that the chains around my ankles were self-imposed, and I already had the keys to the locks. I just had to use them, rather than be a martyr and a victim in my own story.

It's time we all stopped allowing others to make money out of our fear, and started understanding that fear is the greatest obstacle to both our individual and collective wealth and success. Great leaders encourage people to explore alternative possibilities in their lives, which align with their true desires. Great leaders do not coerce others into giving them money, their time or even loyalty. A collective needs to be free to choose, in order to be their own authentic selves. When people, and groups of people, are inspired to explore and participate in new possibilities that spring from the power of love, not fear, their lives can become so much more vibrant and enjoyable, and an evolved leader understands this.

Every individual, organisation, community, or nation has the capacity and opportunity to embrace more of what their hearts desire, and they can do this when they face their fears and convert what they learn into wisdom. Self-care and self-empowerment are powerful forces that can propel them to this amazing place of freedom and enjoyment. We can all have an amazing ride, once we begin to surf on our own wave of joy.

Fear is the greatest policeman of our own limitations. It has a gun to our heads and, unfortunately, we are the ones loading the bullets and pulling the trigger.

Picture a football match where you are both the attack and the defence. Despite all your endeavours, every time you go forward you will block your own ability to score. This is what fear does to our own lives.

The fact is, no one needs to restrain another, or other groups of human beings – because when they live in enough fear, they restrain themselves!

Our task as a population of intelligent beings is to wake up to the illusions and self-imposed restrictions created by fear. Wise leaders will show the way for this, and will give all who they lead the licence to follow their example.

When a leader prioritises the well-being of people over popularity, love over fear, and peace over conflict, great progress is possible. Highly evolved leaders can shepherd their people to a better experience, even if it means substantial change must take place. This is where true strength lies.

Isn't it time we all achieved greater autonomy in our lives? Highly aware leaders can show us the way like a beacon in the night.

## 4.8: Unity Over Separation

### Our Shrinking World

As humankind has evolved, our access to greater technology has made it easier for people to be in contact with each other. As a result, there is a truism in the statement that the world is getting smaller.

However, contact is not the same as connection. Many people today now complain about feeling less connected to others. Our commitment to work, financial pressures, and growing competition in many walks of life (as the populations of the world have risen) have tended to allow us less time to authentically connect with each other with open hearts.

I grew up in a Sydney suburb called Normanhurst, and the people on the street where I lived were in constant contact. As a rule, this type of community closeness has waned in the last few decades, particularly in cities.

The same goes for the business world. When I started work in the 1980s, there seemed to be far less daily pressures on employees. This changed greatly over the following years, as I experienced my own career unfold.

The fact is, we have become victims of our own drive, and the pressure to achieve material possessions. Money seems to matter more than community, more than love, and more than self-awareness. Our obsession with money has led many to be focused on the transaction activity that takes place in their lives, or their business. At least this is what our behaviours suggest.

Wouldn't it be great to have more time to spend with each other, to feel the deep connections unity can bring forth? It is possible, with a few simple shifts in perspective.

## When We Flow, We Grow

Great things in our world have been achieved through collectives of like-minded people working for the same outcome. The project to put the first man on the moon in 1969 resulted from the combined efforts of 400,000 people. It wasn't just done by a handful of famous astronauts and a command centre.

Advanced leaders know that the combined intelligence of a collective of people is far greater than the intelligence of standalone individuals, such as themselves or a limited selection of leaders. Toxic leaders have egos convincing them that they know more than the collective they lead, and without them the team would not succeed.

When a leader encourages their collective to share diverse ideas in an environment that emphasises equality and mutual respect, the energy and intelligence of that combined team can flow with tremendous intent and power in every direction. The combined power of a motivated collective all working or playing together, without fear, is transformative, and creates a myriad of previously untapped possibilities. Great leaders understand the power of diversity and tap into its creative power. When a collective recognises that all in the team have their own unique experiences, abilities, and skills, it can bring them together as one force, and the power of unity can be astounding.

Thus truly great leaders understand that a black and white perspective is actually detrimental for themselves and their collective. They instead embrace the colour that is provided by differing perspectives and truths, and use this colour to paint a clear picture, in their mind, of the best way forward.

On the contrary, when a leader thinks their view is the right and only view, and refuses to truly listen to the perspectives of those they serve, the possibilities for collective inspiration narrow substantially. Instead decisions may well be based on seniority, or numbers, or the loudest voice in the room. This is hardly a decision-making method filled with wisdom.

Fluidity and freedom allow human intelligence and innovation to flourish and flow. Put human beings in an environment where they cannot express their true talents, because they are laden with rules and cornered by restrictions, and human spirits can become compressed. Rules put people in boxes and create segregation, taking away their autonomy and right to free expression.

To truly allow a unified force of diverse human energy to come together for purpose, a leader must drop the power-play that many leaders are conditioned to exhibit. They must learn to live without 'yes people', who simply learn to follow the views of the most senior leaders, where they can feel safe and secure.

In the same way, if a leader's desire for validation and personal importance outweighs their desire to lead important work and achieve important outcomes, the maximum achievement possible will not be met. Power-hungry leaders may feed on the breadcrumbs of temporary success, but empowered leaders enjoy a much greater feast of outcomes, and share it with everyone involved in an ongoing banquet of success.

## Listening as a Strength

Unity requires an ability to truly listen and consider the various options and alternatives being presented. It is often said that we have two ears and only one mouth for a reason.

The ability to listen is a skill that is not natural for many of us, because as people speak we often merely prepare to talk again and impress others with what we know. If being decisive is perceived as strength, then our minds tell us that, if we can make decisions irrespective of the views of others, we must be very strong.

However, it is truly naïve and arrogant for a leader not to seek the views of others and to properly consider them before deciding. They must have empowerment to make the final decision, but if this is made in isolation – without due regard to the intelligent input of others – the harmony in the collective will diminish.

I wish I had understood this dynamic much earlier in my years as a leader. I was so confident in my own opinions as a young executive that I would attend meetings with others, hear the views of those others, but not really listen to them. I would also hold back on expressing my views because, fundamentally, I had already decided on my own course of action and didn't really want to be challenged on it.

As my awareness grew, my interest and compassion for the views of others also grew, though it did take a number of years for me to develop a more open perspective, and to apply it more fully.

Will you be the type of leader who thinks they own the truth and stifle debate, who follows agendas out of personal bias, and who fails to respect the views of all when making decisions?

Evolved leaders respect, or make peace with, the views of those who they lead, and then makes balanced decisions that are in service of achieving benefits for as many stakeholders as possible.

They don't necessarily need to make sense of the views of all, but hearing them with a peaceful and open heart is a great step along the road to balance and collective happiness. It's a must that will deliver trust!

### The Destructive Power of Separate Identities

As human beings we have learned that to feel safe we need a particular identity, something we can belong to and associate with, and that reinforces our value to the world. It's where our minds find safety. We often don't question these alignments, for we don't see that questioning them is possible or valuable. So we try to find our happiness within these forms of identification, rather than questioning the expectations or assumptions that they create.

As a result, we put down roots in particular nationalities, professions, religions, sexual identities, class and so on. Some of these are real and some are arbitrary. We become the identifications that we place upon ourselves. Our story becomes us. We cling to it.

I have done this myself. I was born into this world as a tall, white, athletic, Catholic, Australian male. This gave me much advantage and opportunity throughout my life; particularly given the education standards I was afforded and the career opportunities that education brought to my life. But the reality is that these identities in no way made me superior to anyone else. They were just labels applied by my mind and by the minds of others.

Our propensity to want to be something or someone results in much separation in our lives, for the identifications we think we need can be a falsehood, and can block unity within a collective, as well as with other collectives and individuals who identify themselves in other ways. At its most extreme, this is how wars start between nations, and conflicts start within communities. It's 'us' against 'them', whereas surely 'we' must endure. We perceive differences that others exhibit to ourselves, and assess them to be 'bad' in many cases. We think we must compete and win, and that those who are unlike us stand in our way. We tell ourselves that if we compete today, we will get the spoils down the track. When we identify in some way with a particular identity or set of beliefs, we are prone to judge, and not accept the views and perspectives of others, who could or do disagree with us. This propensity to judge others harshly, and with self-righteousness, blocks the natural flow of tolerance and collaboration within and between collectives, and in turn limits possibilities to be borne out of the richness of differing perspectives.

At our very core we are ultimately all the same. We are equal, no matter what we look like, or where we were born, where we work, or whoever we identify as having become. Our hearts know that this is the case. Being different is not a problem within itself. It's the act of using this differentiation in the name of competition and conflict that ultimately creates suffering, stifles free thinking, and limits our ability to create a more harmonious and unified world.

Respecting uniqueness is 'step one' on the path to unity and the creation of new possibilities. Great leaders unite, they don't separate, for this is where they sense true greatness lies for any collective or community that they lead.

## 4.9: Who Cares, Wins!

A key ingredient missing in many leaders is care – care for their people.

Many leaders care about results or time. They care about how others might see them or how popular they are. They care about their rewards, and their perceived level of importance.

But highly evolved leaders care about the people they lead, as much as they do about anything else, including themselves. People, profits, our planet, and purpose must be balanced and in alignment for true 'success' to arise. A caring leader considers them all constantly.

Caring for people as a leader has become a lost art because of the paradigms within which leaders today are forced to operate. Care has become the victim of circumstances, including the perspective that: to care is to be weak. Like it or not our conditioning has programmed many to see caring leaders as less likely to win. As a society, we often view aggressive leaders as strong, and compassionate leaders as weak.

The opposite is true! Peacemakers are leaders of significant substance; whereas leaders who believe in war over peace are the absolute epitome of weakness – they do not understand the value of people's lives and happiness!

It's time we elevated peace and love as important aspects of leading through care. This might make many leaders feel uncomfortable, for they are subconsciously conditioned to believe in the power of competition over compassion, and assertiveness over care.

Nevertheless, the leaders of the future will be empowered from within, or in other words: from their hearts. To do important things, the care of people must be given due regard, for it's people who truly do most of the real work. And these people have feelings and emotions. We need to care for them, for all to thrive.

## The Wealth of Care

Individuals who feel cared for are more creative, productive, loyal, and devote more time and energy to their collective's success. Doesn't this make sense? If you're happy in your family, of course you want the family to thrive! If you're happy at work, of course you want the business to thrive!

According to a 2022 report entitled '17 Employee Engagement Statistics that Matter the Most', 74% of employees in the US were actively looking for new employment due to poor management and bad work experiences. Those businesses with higher staff engagement had:

- Lower turnover
- Substantial increases in productivity (17% on average)
- Higher motivation
- Higher profitability (17% on average), and
- More discretionary effort by workers.

On the other hand, low staff engagement led to:

- Employees feeling overworked
- Lower morale
- Higher absenteeism
- Staff feeling like they can't recharge their energy
- Higher staff complaints
- More frequent workplace safety issues
- Lower productivity
- More difficult customer experiences
- Declining sales
- Diminishing company reputations and
- Lower financial profits

Although this particular survey may date, its findings and conclusions will no doubt persist in substance. Happy people produce. This is not new news, but leaders who embody this knowing are all too rare. They get distracted by outputs, not inputs.

When you lead people and show them that you care about them, and that their well-being is a key priority, you will receive great loyalty and care in return. The returns in terms of effort and commitment are always extraordinary, because people crave to be truly cared for and to contribute to a team. What goes around comes around as they say. Karma at play!

The leaders of too many collectives subconsciously view individuals as commodities to be exploited for their own benefit. Treating people as commodities is perverse and its effects can be inverse. Even if people are contributing diligently to the collective good, their individual well-being is equally as important, if not more.

Remember, every action has an equal and opposite reaction!

So, if a collective only ever expects to receive the blood, sweat and tears of its people without giving back in equal measure, loyalty will be lost, and exits will take place. Families will separate. Groups will disband. Businesses will dissolve.

I clearly remember one business that had instigated a number of cost-cutting measures, which were particularly brutal on the workforce. Staff were told to be at their desks every Monday morning at precisely 9.00am – to witness the next wave of employees made redundant or otherwise exited. This went on for weeks. It was soul-destroying on everyone, including the leaders, and incredibly disrespectful to staff. Those selected to leave were marched out the door by 10.00am, with their personal belongings in hand. Needless to say, staff morale was soon very low.

You might find yourself working in a business with low morale if your workplace has:

- A disregard for work-life balance.

- Limited investment in staff well-being, particularly when times are tough.
- Uninspiring and vague communication.
- Unclear enunciation of purpose and priorities.
- Inequality of remuneration and opportunity.
- An obsession with financial profits over purpose, the planet, and people's lives.
- A lack of care and compassion for people.
- A cursory interest in the expansion and development of workers, despite this being core to our very nature.
- A competitive environment that pits staff against each other for opportunities and rewards, leading to a general lack of collaboration and a desire to control information and ideas.
- An obsession with appearing to be perfect and all knowing, leading to image projection and protection above all else.
- A focus on the organisation being the best in its industry, rather than being the best it can truly be.

## 4.10: Encouraging Both Forms of Intelligence

We have grown up in a world that rewards knowledge and information. From a young age, most of us are taught the power of our memories and logical minds. Our minds have a great ability to store facts and figures, and the better we do this at school, the more marks we receive. At school, more value is also attributed to subjects like mathematics, history, and science, which are less intuitive and more logically based. Intuitive, creative subjects like music, drama, and art are less valued, and generally only gifted people participate in them because they see them as possible career paths.

This might at first seem like common sense – after all, school is supposed to prepare us for our chosen career paths. But what if school instead prepared us for life? What if it not only taught us the maths we need to make our tax returns and balance our budget, but also how to offset our stress with creative pursuits that bring enrichment to our lives. What if lessons in the creative arts weren't only for career artists, but offered as enrichment activities for everyone? Even just once a term? We all need to express ourselves and to feel self-actualised. These aspects of life may sit at the top of Maslow's Hierarchy of Needs, but they are still very much there and very much necessary – for good reasons.

Yet, because of this segregation at school and beyond, many of us lose sight of the value of creativity, and thus our intuition. As a consequence, we also lose the art of feeling into a problem or decision, using our body as an indicator of that preferred decision. To do this, is to use what is often referred to as 'gut feel'. Our gut feel is truly a relay of information from the teacher within us – our subconscious intuition.

Great leaders can use both forms of decision-making to decide what to do in any given situation. First, they feel into a decision and allow their gut-feel to tell them whether a decision has merit. This is the best place to start. If the gut says 'no', this is a sign that proceeding down a particular path is most likely not right.

The intelligence within us gives us the courage to make the most potent decisions. It gives us the courage from within to make certain decisions. This is pure en-couragement.

But it doesn't stop there. Intuition is first base, but it is best supplemented by the powerful logic of the mind, to complete the analysis needed to finalise a decision. This might normally include analysis and/or case studies to present the positives and negatives of available options, though these can also be limited by the preconditioned views of the author constructing them, and if they are of course only written from the logical mind, they can also be prone to mistakes and exaggeration.

As I progressed in my own career as a leader, I learned to make many decisions quickly from my intuition. These intuitive decisions got stronger and stronger as I learned to feel into the messages coming from my body, and to trust them deeply. This was at odds with some of the analytical cultures I worked in, and people found it curious. However, it never failed me when I trusted it fully.

### Training for Split-Second Accurate Assessments

Bruce Lipton is an American developmental biologist noted for his views on epigenetics, or the study of how behaviours and the environment can change the way our genes or DNA work. In his book *The Biology of Belief*, Mr Lipton puts forward the view that beliefs control human biology more than our DNA and inheritance. Lipton's contentious claims have not received the full attention they deserve from mainstream science, but his following is growing.

Mr Lipton has shown that the intelligence available in your intuition is infinitely faster than the computing power of your mind, and more accurate! It's also free to use. No contractors or technology required! In short, intuition does the same work in split-seconds that our minds can procrastinate to assess.

Many of us, particularly men, have unfortunately lost touch with this powerful assessment tool within our bodies. We have learned not to listen to the powerful force that is our feelings. This inner knowing or power-within is all-knowing, and if you learn to use it and not ignore it, you will never look back.

The empowered leader knows that their true power comes primarily (but not exclusively) from within them. Our intuition is connected to infinite possibilities, unlike the human mind, which works from memories and learned logic.

It's just a matter of listening to the messages and trusting them, like we do with Google!

### A Team of Intuits

An advanced leader will encourage others to trust their intuition when making decisions.

We often end up becalmed in life by a propensity to overanalyse things, especially when our intuition is relatively immediate and available. Analysis paralysis is a common term used to describe this situation.

Many times in my corporate career I saw decisions taking long periods of time to be made, because leaders wanted long drawn-out analyses and business cases before they would commit to a particular direction. They also wanted the agreement of multiple people before they would commit. To me, the decisions often felt obvious, as my gut had made the same decisions in a matter of seconds or minutes, and I trusted this more as the years unfolded. Yes, sometimes I needed business cases, albeit rarely.

If you want to be the leader you are capable of being, it's a great idea to learn to access your intuition and to feel into a decision, and to encourage others in your collective to do the same. It's here that great possibilities can be found, quickly and easily.

Don't think the decision, until you have already felt it. I have drilled this wisdom into my children, and it can apply to all parts of one's life. Every part!

True authority is found within yourself. It does not need to come from others!

## AI Versus II

The mega-trend known as artificial intelligence (or AI) is sweeping the world at present and promises to change the very core of our existence. Whether this change is positive or negative, or a combination of both, will be determined by the way we as humans use this powerful new tool. It's ours to harness and control, not the other way around, and it's our senior leaders in business and government who will have the greatest influence on where this all ends up.

The very description of AI tells me that its usage has deep limitations, for it is artificial by its very nature. These systems, unlike living creatures, don't have a soul and never can, so their computing power is likely to just speed up the current forces of human IQ on society. These systems will mirror our societal beliefs and priorities, including any conscious or sub-conscious limiting beliefs we hold.

It's critical that we manage this transformative era well, or what may eventuate from this new powerful force could be highly destructive to our lives, given how exponentially AI computing power is growing, and what it is capable of doing for or to us.

If intuitive intelligence or II is employed to direct the AI we create then imagine the positive outcomes that could flow very quickly from this potent union of intelligent forces.

This situation is shaping as a massive challenge for mankind to manage in the years ahead. This will require wise leadership of the highest order for there is much at stake.

## 4.11: Standing for Transformation, Not Information

Evolution and transformation are key places where advanced leaders play.

We live in the information age, where data abounds and grows every day. It was estimated in 2020 that the world had created 64.2 zettabytes of data on computers across the world, and this is now growing at around 15 zettabytes a year. A zettabyte is equal to a trillion gigabytes of data. Let's just say, it's a lot.

Humankind has created access to all this data because our minds constantly crave it. The mind believes that there is safety in information. Information, they say, is power and/or money.

There is no shortage of data available to a leader if they wish to access it. You no longer need to go to the local library to consult expensive encyclopaedias, as I did growing up. The internet provides it all in seconds, as no doubt will new forms of artificial intelligence.

In a way there is so much data that, in fact, we are losing our ability to see the 'wood for the trees'. Simplicity is getting lost in the flow of data and information. We are drowning in it. We know so much about our world, yet it doesn't stop us from wrecking it. If we listened to our hearts, however, and not so much of our minds – which cannot help but be distracted by the safe allure of more data – we would instantly know what we have to do to save the planet.

Too much information can be the enemy of intuition.

In my career, I experienced this constant overload of information first-hand. The amount of reading I was asked to do was incredible at times. For example, it was not unusual to receive over 500 pages of information for a board meeting only a few days away, and to have to create from it intelligent questions or contributions for discussion.

Producing these papers was an industry in itself, and left the readers struggling to see key principles needing discussion.

I have great empathy for senior leaders who need to absorb copious quantities of information just to do their daily jobs.

### Transformation is a Job in Itself

Before making a decision, instead of analysing streams of information for the mind, evolved individuals look inside themselves to seek out the instincts of their heart. Such individuals might not like what they find at first, as they might encounter core beliefs that have made their lives more difficult and painful. I have been through this experience myself, which is why I now take great pleasure in assisting others with their own transformations – it can really help to have an experienced mentor by your side as you confront your beliefs and develop a true sense of authenticity.

But with this revelation comes great opportunity, for if a person can transform their life to embrace their heart's desires, they can then express that experience to their collectives and thus inspire them to do the same.

This can involve a substantial amount of inner work and self-reflection, but it is a core element of growing your self-awareness levels.

Some changes are easier than others of course, and most of us have rent or a mortgage to pay, bills and/or debt. So we subrogate our dreams to survive. But I would urge any reader who feels that their life is too stressful and full of obligation to transform, to actually take a step back for a moment and at least consider their options and priorities.

Could they work for themselves or try a new vocation? Do they have a special talent they would love to turn into a job? At the end of the day, we need to be the leaders of our own lives and destinies.

I have changed my own life in a big way to explore such new possibilities. I redesigned my life completely and I'm proud to say that it has made me immeasurably happier. This didn't come without cost, but I accept those as the price I pay for happiness. I am happy, and that's worth everything. Life is a series of choices, possibilities, and trade-offs. I am happy that happiness is the result of mine.

Carving this path is not easy for anyone, but it is both natural and can be exhilarating.

To get there simply requires a higher state of self-awareness, strength, resilience, and the choice to question 'what is'.

Am I really where I want to be? What do I love?

Ultimately, those who stand up to transform end up understanding the true importance of happiness to the world around them, and the need for this to be potent and progressive. They will understand how happiness gives them real purpose and meaning, and their future decision-making will be wiser and more masterful because of it. They will have found that inner spark that enables them to be present, and receive broad perspectives from all who surround them.

This awareness is more valuable to any evolved individual than information, and is a great core trait of the evolved leader.

### Self-Transformation is Infectious

Once a leader opens the inner doorway to this awareness, the rest of their collective can follow suit.

Self-awareness, once seen as a priority, can allow all in a collective to grow at their own pace. The leader will set the tone from the so-called top.

### The 360 Experiment

When I worked as an executive in business, I was often bemused that feedback on leaders was kept so private, and not often shared. I always shared mine with my team, in full honesty, and thanked them for their feedback. In fact, I emailed it in full to all the people who I led, with my commitments that I had undertaken to follow to address any significant areas of improvement raised. The tendency for leaders to keep this kind of feedback so hush-hush always told me that they found it difficult to be seen as imperfect, and truly did not see the power of embracing vulnerability in their leadership transformations.

What a shame so many opportunities to grow are lost by modern leaders, who do not understand that self-awareness, and their commitment to expansion and growth for all, is the greatest gift they can give to the people they lead, and to themselves.

## 4.12: Communicating for Trust

Advanced leaders win the hearts and minds of those they lead with integrity in their communications.

All too often, leaders communicate to get what they want, not to inform those who they serve to then give them a choice. They may in fact be serving their own agenda as a priority. This is particularly evident in political speeches.

Self-interest in a leader distorts the message and provides false hope, for it may not have the right intention behind it, or it may be self-serving. This promotes distrust.

An advanced leader is self-centred, aware and aligned with the truth of a situation, and seeks to promote trust as a priority. This is their natural way.

### Trust Versus Control

Most collectives want to trust that their leaders are there for the benefit of all. They listen intently to their leaders' communications, for they crave leaders who act on their unified behalf. They want to trust their leader, and be trusted by their leader.

This two-way street of trust is, however, often overtaken by a highway of control, leading straight into distrust. This is typically the fault of the leader, but can be contributed to by the collective. We all have the power to feel when a leader is acting with integrity or not, though we often ignore it. Over time, many of us have been conditioned into a place of subservience to our leaders. We can be apathetic to their decisions, because it's easier to just conform. We do not challenge openly out of habit, and because we feel afraid to step up and speak out. We often cannot trust our leader to respond with authentic compassion and an openness to the collective well-being.

I experienced this several times in my career, working for controlling leaders, with whom it was difficult to debate matters. The temptation was to give up for the sake of self-preservation. But such an approach would have been energetically expensive.

When a leader acts with integrity, the collective they serve will *feel* the genuine leadership present, and trust its intention. They *know* they can openly challenge their leader if need be, without reprisal.

When a leader's communications are made with integrity, it is often said that they touch the audience. This is because they truly do. The audience feels the integrity in their bodies. Of course, if a decision does not serve an individual's particular self-interest, they may not like it, but they will at least continue to respect that their leader has acted from their heart, and will feel that genuine intent.

## Communicating in a Crisis

In a genuine crisis, the opportunity for a leader to truly excel rises significantly, as those in the collective are likely to be afraid and look for their leader to show resilience and wisdom.

In a crisis, collectives will want more regular communication, to give them greater certainty or clarity on events or plans. It is human nature to want certainty, particularly in a crisis. We all want to feel safe and secure, or to get back to circumstances that we see as normal.

The word 'normal' can be very misleading of course. Normal often just refers to the 'devil we know', or circumstances with which we are familiar. It may not be a circumstance we are truly happy with, more just accustomed to experiencing.

If a leader can't give certainty, then they should not, for this is likely to lead to widespread disappointment among the collective once a different outcome eventuates. We see this all too often in politics, particularly in run-ups to elections. We see it in families too, whose leaders over-promise or play down the significance of events.

People want to hear truth, above all else, and to feel a sense of hope – even if they hear that a realistic solution is still being developed.

They also want their leaders to be more visible in a crisis. Leaders who retract in tough times, for fear of not getting it right, are likely to lose the faith of their collectives.

From my experience, this is common as leaders bunker down, or perhaps restrict their communications to written communications, such as email.

Evolved leaders, however, understand the power of integrity in their communications with collectives, and the purpose of those communications to create harmony.

The leaders in all walks of life have different audiences to communicate with, and this can also be challenging. For example, in big corporates, there are multiple stakeholders including staff, suppliers, customers, regulators and shareholders, just to name a few. Sophisticated communications are then needed to reach those different categories of stakeholders.

However, whoever is being communicated with, the golden rule needs to apply, that: leaders need to be in full integrity and compassion, be honest, and if possible provide hope and remove fear. In other words, they need to communicate to their people in the same way they would want to be communicated to.

### Corrosive Self-Interest

Self-interest has created a world where the interpretation of facts can be distorted to drive the outcomes people think will serve them. However, self-interest is a corrosive energy that can drive gossip and misinformation across a collective.

It is important for a true leader to rise above any self-interest, and instead inspire collectives to speak the truth and communicate across the team, without the fear of hurting individual members.

The most powerful collectives speak truth without attacking individuals or attaching blame without sufficient compassion. There may of course be circumstances where speaking the full truth is not caring or legal, and needs to be carefully managed in terms of who has access to it.

But otherwise evolved leaders stand for truth with compassion, honesty without judgement, and communication without gossip and politics.

## 4.13: The Responsibility to Believe in Autonomy

Autonomy is a key aspect of life that many of us trade-off for security or 'perceived' forms of success. It is aligned with the human right to choose our own life and to be free.

Evolved leaders stand in their own autonomy as a priority, because it is more important to them than being rewarded or validated. They know that autonomy means taking responsibility, and accountability, for things that matter; yet never taking the blame for things that are unfairly directed at them.

In this place, a collective can become fully capable of controlling its own destiny, and therefore achieve autonomy.

Autonomy is a knowing, and must come from within. It must be felt to be real. No one can give it to a leader, they must establish it within themselves, and then step into it. This doesn't mean you need to be alone, or be your own boss. It is a state of mind and not determined by circumstances or a story. Autonomy dwells in your heart and is therefore inherent in us all. It can be sidestepped by the adroit controlling mind, and often is, as such a mind trades off autonomy for safety.

But a true leader who is autonomous, knows who they are. They know that if they give in and take unfair blame, or fail to act with integrity or honesty in any situation, their sense of self will be scarred by the experience. They are powerful enough to withstand the temptation to be manipulated, and will push back before they significantly erode their sense of self by giving in to others inappropriately.

Early in my career, I had a few situations that, in hindsight, should have seen me resign, rather than cling to my position, because I disagreed in principle with an organisation's values, strategy, and direction. Fortunately I learned this lesson as I progressed, but only after a few missteps.

An evolved leader brings their sense of autonomy to the collective that they lead. They are both a key source of inspiration and motivation, and the team's protector. An inspiring leader won't allow the team's reputation to be diminished by unfair criticism or comments. When the empowered leader protects their team, they protect themselves as well.

At the same time, as mentioned above, a leader should bring an honesty to the team that allows valid criticism to be heard and dealt with in a constructive way. Blame should never be borne by anyone, or any collective, unless they have at least had the full ability to respond to a situation. Any leader that puts themselves or their team in a position of taking unfair criticism for a matter, is leading the team into an energetic or moral devaluation.

It takes great courage and strength to preserve autonomy, but once the belief in its importance is understood within a collective, there is no looking back.

## 4.14: Being Energised, Not Timed

Time is in control of much of our lives. We often say we are time poor or short of time. We treat time as a commodity in our vernacular, which reflects the belief that we can possess time, that it is something we need more of. Our mentality tells us it's in short supply, because we only live for so long. We are mortal beings and know we will eventually die. Therefore, our time on Earth is finite.

With this in mind, most collectives are ruled by the concept of and commitments to time. People experience great stress as the rigours of deadlines take their toll. It has even become a 'badge of honour' to be busy in our lives. In business I used to hear people say every day how busy they were. It validates us to be in demand by others, because therein lies security or safety in the continuation of our present situation. We perceive that it's better to be stressed and earning money, than freer but less financially rewarded. Many of us rank security significantly higher in priority than freedom and happiness. I did once, but no more!

This is of course a trade-off we all get to make. It's our choice, and a choice we can truly own, though our conditioning often stops us from seeing the possibilities. We will never get any more time in any given day than 24 hours of course. So all we can really do is decide how best to use our time. The answer is obvious: we should use it wisely. So why don't we make more conscious decisions around time?

In my 50s, I finally made this choice. Despite having high-income earning capacity, I made the decision to choose my personal freedom over money, use my time differently and thereby embrace the opportunity to write books and develop my consulting business, to assist both individuals and collectives transform their personal, social and work lives. It has been incredibly rewarding. I feel energised every day, and grateful to be alive.

Indeed, the universe itself does not work off time, it works off energy. Things evolve as energy coalesces, not when the alarm goes off. Time is a man-made concept, although it has practical uses.

The universe has a plan, so perhaps we don't need another one for everything we do! But this takes trust and patience, which are often in short supply.

### It's About Time for Leadership Wisdom

Many individuals who are not in leadership roles feel more powerless than their leaders when it comes to controlling time. There is much basis for this belief.

Leaders as a rule set the agenda. In business, leaders set the culture, and this often influences the pressures exerted on employees. It may impact on the internal processes, and meeting and email practices that staff are expected to comply with. In families, it's often the leaders who determine when it's time to do something, or not. Government leaders set deadlines, which can often be seen by many as too slow, with 'red tape' and bureaucracy frustrating the public.

Many leaders, particularly in business, want things done as fast as possible so that it reflects well on them. This again can be propelled by self-interest, or perhaps it has been an edict from above or by a regulator.

Evolved leaders, however, work from energy first, and translate that into time and deadlines where appropriate. They do not do it the other way around, unless they have to of course. In deciding what needs to be done by when, they will take account of a myriad of factors, such as:

- The resources and capabilities of the collective
- The true priority of the process or project
- The impact of the event on the collective's well-being, and
- Any alternative use of resources

These kinds of factors are considered as a priority, rather than as an outcome that will make the leader look good.

Where there is no need to put excess time pressure on people, why do it? It may just make the collective feel used and abused, and may eventually backfire on the leader, as well as the people they lead. In my career I often sacrificed my personal life to meet what, in hindsight, were unreasonable deadlines. I met them even if I didn't get to sleep or go home for days on end. Looking back these were unfair experiences, and probably contributed to my divorces and health issues. I'm sure many readers have experienced these same pressures.

Advanced leaders understand that people are a part of nature, and therefore their energy needs to be responsibly managed. Their energy rises and falls like the waves upon the sea.

Stress, if it's excessive, translates into unhappiness, and too much time pressure for too long is not good for the ease by which people exist. And if we create unease, we create disharmony for individuals and collectives.

## 4.15: Balancing the 4 Ps

As discussed above, to be successful as a leader, there are four things that must be properly balanced: purpose, people, profit, and the needs of our planet.

We are currently out of balance in many levels of society, and the balance of these factors has been arguably lost for centuries. As it stands people, the planet, and purpose are often sacrificed for a focus on financial profit. Our planet is suffering from our obsession with consuming and owning material things.

When the planet, people and purpose are compromised for financial profit by those in power, the door is thrown open for corruption, unhappiness, and unease. We have seen this play out many times in life. Corruption has been in evidence in many structures, such as in governments and business organisations, over the centuries.

Potent leaders of the future need to restore this balance to achieve a better equilibrium, which will recognise and enforce the importance of each, while allowing the long-term dominance of none. It has to start inside the leader. They need to 'walk the talk' before they can expect others to do the same.

When purpose and people are key drivers of any collective and their leaders, incredible creativity and inspiration can be experienced by those involved, and this can create great profits for all. When people, purpose, profit, and the love of our planet, are all in alignment and of a sensible relative value, you have tremendous potential for sustainable creativity to step forth. This balance is fully supportive of unity.

Advanced leaders are truly interested in more than money. Money does not validate them or give them the illusion of power, because their hearts have no need for power and greed is not on their agenda. They step forth and lead with the well-being of the collective as their priority. They know that they are just a part of that collective, not the only part that matters. Great leaders are powered from within, not from that which exists outside themselves. Nothing defines them for they are already defined by integrity and authenticity. They are defined by them-selves, with 'self' being the key word. They know who and what they are. Their core burns with a desire to take their team on a meaningful and expansive journey.

Of course no collective, business, society, or organisation in our modern world can exist and thrive without the energy of sufficient money, in whatever form it takes. However, this financial viability is enhanced and takes on untold levels of possibility when profit, purpose and people are all in concert, and that score is one of equality and harmony, enabling us to stop exploiting our planet and instead restore its health.

None of us can survive, let alone thrive, without our 'planet' Earth. Ongoing manipulation of the planet will eventually lead to the other Ps becoming irrelevant or at threat.

Apart from sunlight, everything we are or need to survive comes from our planet. We are one with it, not separate from it. We do not own it. We are not landholders, just renters for the course of our lives. The planet holds us in its love. We do not hold it.

When we die, our bodies are returned to the planet. Ashes to ashes, dust to dust.

A core issue lies in the illusion that humanity believes it is separated from the planet. Thus we fail to see that all in this world are linked and are one, including our relationship to the Earth. The truth is that we are part of nature, not above, below, or separated from it. We are it. It is us. Indigenous peoples seem to comprehend this. Still we persist in separating the consequence of our actions for the planet, from the consequences for ourselves. This is clearly a short-term way of thinking, and by all measures is false.

Most of the time, this distorted way of thinking drives us to get our Ps out of whack. When our primary purpose is to make money, this does not bode well for the planet or most people. Thus the question we need to ask ourselves is: how we can make profits that serve the planet and its people – and not just a minority of people, as is the case at present. Everyone matters.

This is the only way to true sustainability.

At present the world is besieged with a huge gap between the mega-wealthy and the impoverished. And this gap is continuing to rise. It became even greater during the Coronavirus crisis, with many business owners joining the ranks of the mega-rich, and the mega-rich becoming the mega-mega rich. Many of these business owners benefitted from the growth of internet shopping due to pandemic lockdowns, and new mega trends across the world, such as green energy and electric vehicle trends.

Those with wealth can then use their money to create more wealth, exacerbating the gap between the rich and poor. The poor struggle to get out of the circumstances they are in, for they may have limited or no funds to invest towards a better future. The wealthy just get wealthier.

I am not criticising those with wealth. Most likely they have taken risks and created value for society, and that society has rewarded them with significant wealth. But when is enough, enough? Shouldn't something trigger them to share their wealth at some point, even if by way of higher taxes?

The following is a sobering chart, extracted from a paper issued by the world Economic Forum in December 2021. It shows the share of wealth and income of the respective economic tiers of people in the world.

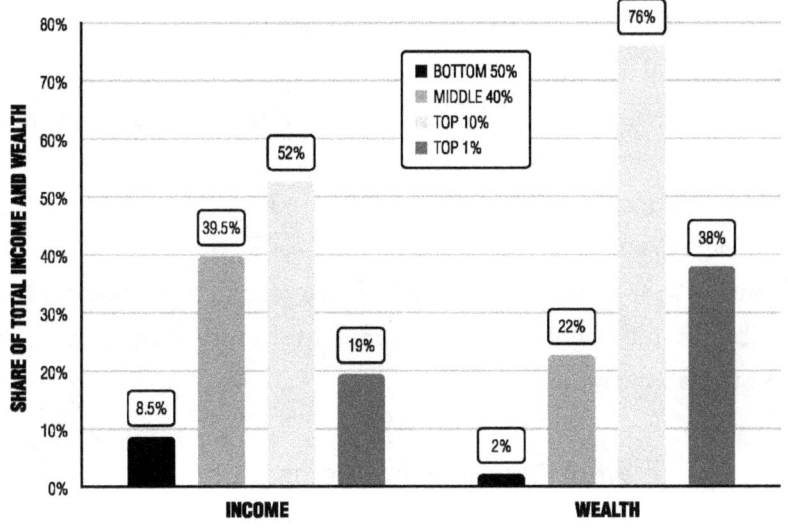

Figure 2: Global Income and Wealth Inequality 2021
Source: wir2022.wid.world/methodology

This chart shows that in 2021, the top 10% of people by wealth held 76% of the world's wealth and earnt 52% of global income.

By contrast the bottom 50% owned only 2% of the world's wealth and earned only 8.5% of its total income. Let's not forget that the bottom 50% is about four billion people.

The report also noted that in 2021 the known billionaires of the world owned 3% of global wealth. This had tripled over the previous 25-year period.

Another interesting finding of the report was that, of the global income inequality that existed in 2020, 32% of this inequality was represented by the gap between rich and poor countries, and the remaining 57% existed within countries – between segments of the population. So the inequality exists both within and between countries.

These wealth and income gaps can be tempered to a degree by taxation policies and welfare systems. However, a redistribution of wealth is more likely to arise if belief structures change, and the wealthy see greater benefit from helping their fellow humans in a more substantial way.

One wonders what awareness would need to be triggered, and by what, to bring this into reality.

Many people dream of the kind of wealth that the mega-rich attain, but although it's theoretically possible for all, the reality is most of us will never achieve it. We are unfortunately disconnected from significant wealth by opportunity.

But we should never say 'never'. Every moment brings forth fresh possibilities for change and advancement for us all. And wise leaders make this all the more possible.

## What Goes Around, Comes Around

As mentioned above, one of the greatest problems the world has at present, is that we believe we are separate from others. This leads us to believe that we can be separated from the consequences of our actions. In other words, we can do whatever we want as long as it's legal and we can get away with it.

If it won't directly impact me, then I may as well do it because I won't be harmed.

But this thinking is false, and many will tell you that it is contrary to the principle of Karma or: what goes around, comes around.

We are all energetically connected to each other, and even if you can't get your mind around this truth, there is one big common thing we are all undeniably connected to, and that is the planet.

Many people are invested in businesses for financial profit, such as manufacturing which can have a significant negative impact on the planet, primarily through pollution. Because these businesses believe in separation, and many don't care about the negative consequences of their actions for others, as they are not directly impacted, they continue to do harm to our shared home, Earth.

We all breathe the same air, all the oceans of the world are connected, and weather patterns don't stand still, so we are all ultimately in their path. We all sit on the tectonic plates of the Earth, which push against each other as physical pressure builds upon the planet. When pressure becomes too much, beware! The widespread impact of earthquakes, volcanos and big storms can be devastating for any people in their path of destruction.

Did you know that there are currently an estimated 1350 potentially active volcanos in the world and 500 of these have erupted in human history? And these are just the ones above ground. Scientists believe that there are thousands beneath the sea and probably many more we don't even know exist.

Mother Nature will not tolerate human beings putting financial profit and consumerism ahead of the planet forever. We need to wake up to the illusion that we can abuse the Earth, and it will put up with it, without an equal and opposite reaction. Our decisions all have consequences. We are gradually starting to see this, but getting a true collective approach to addressing it has thus far been too difficult for world leaders, although some steps are now in progress.

When you consider that the world as we know it has been around for thousands of years, and for many of those years our ancestors walked before us, can you imagine how ruined our world would now be if they had polluted the planet like we do, the so-called modern inhabitants? It would be a disaster, that's for sure; and possibly human beings would be extinct by now.

## 4.16: Reshaping the Meaning of Success

As mentioned above, there are four Ps that need to be balanced. A core purpose of any collective leadership is to get these happening in the right order of priority, at any point in time.

The false illusion we have created in our lives is that material wealth gives us the best access to happiness and fulfilment. Our society tends to value people by the size of their house, the type of car they drive, where they live, what job they have and how attractive their partner is.

It's all a story at the end of the day, and the wise leaders of the world know this. Sure, money gives us the energy to live a fulfilling life, and is therefore important; but it is not the experiences our hearts truly seek. It just funds them.

We will always need a form of exchange as a society. We are unlikely to ever go back to carrying bags of wheat or rice on our backs or swapping cows in order to trade. But we have become so obsessed with keeping up the appearance of success that we don't often discuss what success actually is for us. We simply devote our lives to working, so we can acquire expensive food, wine, hotels, houses, and overseas holidays as our reward, then wonder why we are still unhappy.

I left the corporate world as an employee in 2019, to develop my own business and became an author. Since then, I have re-evaluated my life and realised what real happiness is to me. This has led me to a much simpler life. This of course may not be what others want, but I now find no meaning whatsoever in many of the luxuries I previously sought. Other things have greater value, such as:

- Being in nature
- Staying fit
- Being with family and friends
- Being in silence and learning about myself

I could go on, but you get my point. My story no longer fits the normal mould of success, but I don't care because it has made me happier on the inside, and opened the door to greater possibilities for me.

The advanced leaders of the future will be able to see through the false illusion of the modern world, where money and financial profit are the pinnacles of success. Of course, to some people, this may be their conscious choice and that is acceptable. But is it actually us making that conscious choice, or following the subconscious herd in a daze?

In all walks of life, leaders can step back and ask people what will truly make them happy, and design collectives that can better deliver these attributes to the lives of those in that collective. This can also work for romantic relationships and families.

In their hearts, people may prefer to work more at home, spend more time with family, or be given more leave, for example. People may prefer to value fun over work commitments, which may make them too tired or stressed to really enjoy life.

You can lead yourself to such a life – free of chains and full of self-autonomy. However, ideally, we need more leaders who can see through the illusion and bring life back to a more natural place, where we can be in unison with nature and other fellow human beings, happy and productive at the same time. It just takes awareness and a desire to continuously improve everyone's lives.

Relationships and fun do actually matter more than money to many, and the collectives of the future that don't recognise this could find themselves abandoned as we make the shift into lives based on greater autonomy and freedom. The trend towards working from home, post the Covid-19 pandemic, has contributed greatly to this being recognised by leaders.

## 4.17: Embracing the Inevitability of Rebirths

In our lives, we can often experience what our minds interpret as failure. We are most likely to have set expectations, and not met them. This causes us stress, and we can sometimes find it hard to forgive ourselves, for our perfectionistic tendencies can make us fragile and prone to overreact to what our minds perceive as not good enough.

My life has experienced multiple let downs or 'failures', including the loss of jobs, two divorces, losses of money and health lapses. What got me through it all, although my ego wanted to collapse at times, was my heart and its will to endure.

However much my mind tried to prevent my broken heart from shattering, the power to heal resided within my heart, as it does for all of us, when we surrender to self-love. It took me many years to redefine the events I had seen as failures, and instead see them as opportunities for growth; but the secret to this change began when I started to understand what I had learned from my problems. With every recognition, my awareness rose, and so did my joy. I began to embrace my situation and eventually see the positives that arose from every mishap. From here I was able to let them go with love.

When we see a failure as an adverse event that requires us to start again, we will normally become unhappy and frustrated, for we feel like the energy we gave to a situation or relationship was a waste of time. However, when we learn that from a less than ideal situation, we can not only transform ourselves, but we can change our perception of needing to start again into a rebirth or fresh start, then failure translates into opportunity.

In my case this was personally liberating, and gave me great new hope in my life. I saw my own strength and the resilience in my heart. My inner power helped me to make the most out of every so-called failure, and I became grateful for them, which I know is somewhat unusual.

The same principle applies to leaders and collectives. With eight billion people interacting with each other in the world, all different and at various levels of consciousness, life will never be perfect or work out as any leader or collective might hope. Dysfunction and disruption are inevitable in some form. This is a given that we must accept.

It does of course come with its share of challenges.

It can be incumbent on a great leader to see every event taking place as a gift, be it positive or negative. Gratitude is a powerful emotion that a leader can harness for the good of all in a collective. And gratitude for learning is particularly special! But it is still an encumbrance to deploy consistently, though consistency is a must, because for a collective to really improve or transform itself over time, it must find the good in the bad. This is freedom of the highest order.

There is a special energy in a leader who can find him or herself excited by a challenging situation, and bring to the table a love of learning and advancement, despite the circumstances.

I used to feel the excitement in me rise during difficult circumstances in my career. People often found this to be a curiosity, and so did I for many years, until I realised that my inherent nature was to love change and challenge. I got bored in repetitive situations, and uninspired by the status quo. This has been a gift I cherish, given the level of change my life has now experienced. So I encourage you to ask yourself this: are you here to just accumulate assets, or to grow in wisdom and joy? Wisdom can create assets, but assets can't create wisdom!

Despite my love of change, I have still found that 'starting over' emotionally taxing at times, particularly in my younger years when everyone else seemed to have less ups and downs. My ego was in charge, so I looked at others and compared myself to them. I was afraid I was 'falling behind'.

But if people are in a state of fear, and cannot find the growth potential in a 'failure', their ultimate power to find improvement and inspiration will be truncated. Fear of failure limits the ability of a leader or collective to increase its awareness, and the level of awareness is the ultimate determiner of success.

Would Apple be the company it is today if its co-founder Steve Jobs had not had this mentality, reflected in his own words?

> "Sometimes when you innovate you make mistakes. It is best to admit them quickly, and get on with improving your other innovations."

In 1985, Jobs was fired by Apple; but he reassessed his approach and later reentered Apple to take it to new heights. He did not give up.

Oprah Winfrey once said:

> "Think like a queen. A queen is not afraid to fail. Failure is another steppingstone to greatness."

Oprah had a well-documented difficult childhood, but went on to greatness as a talk show host, and more, because of her evolved awareness and resilience.

JK Rowling, the famous author of Harry Potter, once said:

> "It is impossible to live without failing at something, unless you live so cautiously that you might as well not have lived at all, in which case you have failed by default."

JK Rowling brought great wonder and joy to the world, and the point that she makes about living too cautiously is a powerful one. If you have a great dream or idea, and fail to step into it out of fear, you have arguably failed. If you follow your dream, and it does not work out, at least you tried and gave it your best shot. This experience will no doubt be rich in learnings.

Where would Apple be today if Steve Jobs had not sought to change the way people see a phone?

The secret to greatness can come from constant rebirth. Every day there is a new sunrise, and a new day is birthed. Evolved leaders embrace the energy of rebirth. They know that 'failure' is a great teacher, and they embrace it as a way of taking awareness to new heights.

Of course, too many repeated failures may not be sustainable if it creates too much financial instability or loss of reputation. However, this can also be a matter of perspective.

The greater leaders step into possibility, including the possibility of failure, knowing that higher levels of awareness are the only way to greatness, and to new possibilities beyond what already exists.

Life can sometimes use failure to shunt you back onto the preferred path. Advanced leaders see the power in a path correction and shine their light on the preferred direction for the collectives they lead.

### Letting Go and Letting In

The consequences of failure can often be exacerbated in today's world through the importance we place on reputation. 'Reputation damage' may not have been as brutal in the past when communities were more local by nature. If someone failed, it wasn't announced on mainstream social media platforms around the world, inescapable to the point that it might feel like a death in itself.

Not only that, but we often feel like we have a certain image to maintain, whether we're online or offline. Therefore when we encounter anything that might endanger that image, particularly how we might be regarded within a collective, we become anxious and afraid. If we were to say or do the wrong thing, or appear the wrong way, we can begin to feel like our world is coming to an end. What if others find out we've made a mistake at work, or even lost our job? What if others find out we're struggling financially, or even lose our home? What if our relationships start to deteriorate, we lose our partner or access to our kids?

The proliferation of social media has exacerbated the damage that any loss of reputation can do to a person's psyche. As bad things occur, they can very quickly be splashed around the world for all to see and judge.

The death of our reputations can become crippling for an individual, or a collective of people, and the more evolved leaders understand this dynamic, both within their teams and within the individuals they lead, including themselves. They are sensitive to the perception of less-than-ideal outcomes. They do not frame them as failures but as opportunities to arise or be reborn. The advanced leader does not create victims or martyrs out of a so-called failure. They encourage all involved to accept what has taken place, for it cannot be changed, and this opens the way for their team to rise above it and reach a whole new level.

When we see a failure as a great learning experience in this way, we can transcend the loss of our reputation, the modern version of death, and prevent people from suffering an unnecessary sense of failure or shame. Perhaps in the future, we can be more aptly described as learners, not consumers?

Everything happens for a reason. Admiring a storm and not letting it break you is the best way to experience it. But to do so you need to bend with its forces, because total resistance can be dangerous.

This is where true courage and resilience resides. When you lead in this way, people lose fear, and this will always lead them to higher places of self-confidence, gratitude, and performance. Our egos may tell us to hide from a storm, but our self-esteem can grow from every storm we endure.

Acceptance rather than resistance is the trick to letting go of so-called failures, and to letting new possibilities in.

## 4.18: Relaxing into Who We Are

An advanced leader is one who inspires calm, and calm is a powerful force for creativity, knowing, productivity and new beginnings.

In times of stress, creativity is not completely impossible to find, but it is harder to access. Thus relaxation is the key to creativity, so that creativity can allow for new possibilities, and new possibilities can result in expanded opportunities and awareness.

This relaxation comes from knowing yourself. When we choose to connect to our true selves, and ask questions of truth itself, we access our intuition and enter a place of ease. Our intuition is not mired in memory, but feels free to explore possibility.

Inspiration by its very description comes from the spirit within our hearts. It is not normally the function of a past experience or a thought we heard elsewhere. These just represent thoughts that are part of a story we already know. Inspiration, however, is typically met with a surge of energy from our inner knowing. Our bodies connect us to the energy within our hearts by way of feeling. They are a powerful conduit without which we cannot live. The task of accessing our inner wisdom therefore emanates from the spirit within us, though our minds also play a role – in directing our attention towards our inner enquiries and sensing the meaning of any inspiration we receive.

For a leader to lead through intuition, and therefore to stand in inspiration and ease, they are best placed to do so through the calm consideration of their own inner wisdom. This requires that leaders to be calmly in touch with their feelings, for here in this relaxed state they will find the awareness they seek. This requires them to find space for deep self-reflection and to listen to their hearts through their intuition and feelings. In this place, wisdom is embodied, for in their bodies they feel the inspirations they hunger for.

Imagine a collective where the leader inspires its members to also relax into their own inner wisdom, even if it's only periodically, so that truth has a chance to be heard over the noise emanating from other parts of their activities. Regular down time to feel into the vibration of fresh ideas and new awareness is a great gift that any self-aware leader can bestow upon their team. Then watch the magic unfold! They will ask questions of their heart and wait patiently for the answer, because they know that nature does not work off the time on their wrist, but the energy of the circumstances at hand.

Have you ever felt inspiration come to you when you least expected it? Perhaps you were travelling somewhere, playing sport, or just sitting in nature. Evolved leaders appreciate this powerful source of knowledge, and embrace it.

## 4.19: A Chance to Self-Reflect

Set out in Appendix I is a checklist for readers who want to pause at this stage, and reflect on how the ideas in this book resonate with their own experiences and observations of 'modern' leadership. This, of course, could include your own experiences, if you have already taken on a leadership role.

Self-reflection is a powerful resource that can help us continuously expand, for it is a powerful conduit to higher awareness and wisdom. And it is through gaining wisdom we can live a spectacular life. At this point of your journey, you may therefore want to pause and reflect on how aligned you feel with the concepts put forward so far.

To do this, ask yourself the following questions:

- Would you be inspired to work for a leader who exhibits the kinds of calm and collaborative qualities expressed so far, or do you prefer the more traditional model of leadership that most people have become accustomed to, which promotes competition and moving forward through constant crises?
- Have you had the opportunity to be a part of, or observe, a collective where an advanced leader, as described in this book, has taken their people on a natural journey of expansion and evolution? How did witnessing and experiencing this feel to you?
- Would you get excited by the opportunity to develop your leadership potentialities so you could become a natural leader, like the model leader described in this book?

- Could you commit to such a path and arise as an advanced leader, even if it put you out-of-step with other more traditional leaders, or cost you short-term opportunities, because you know this way of leading is ultimately in the best interests of you and the collectives of which you are a part?
- Do you align with the belief that to truly lead people with authenticity you need to go inward and know yourself first? Would you be prepared to do this in reality? Is this something you would need further guidance on?
- Do you align with the power of concepts critical to advanced leadership including:
    - Promoting unity over separation.
    - Direct and honest communication.
    - Allowing all to be unique within a unified collective.
    - Caring for people rather than just being focused on outcomes.
    - Balancing the 4Ps, not just being caught up in the financial profit motive.
    - The power of forgiveness over blame, learning over outcomes.
    - Embracing fears and learning through them, rather than allowing them to control you and stifle new possibilities in a never-ending sea of risk-management activities.
    - Understanding that all of us are equal in a collective, regardless of the job we do, the responsibilities we hold or the titles we possess. In other words, do you agree that there is no top in any collective, in reality?
    - Relying on intuition to make decisions, not just logic and business cases.
    - The real meaning of integrity in leadership. It's not about understanding the best thing to say, but knowing what truly resonates with your heart and mind in every moment that matters.

- o Understanding the power of down-time in our lives to allow creativity to surface, from which we can all benefit. In other words, sometimes we need to slow down temporarily, in order to speed up in the medium- to long-term.
- o That too much control can ultimately damage a culture, and put a limit on its ability to expand exponentially, for control is devoid of love and therefore intimidates creativity.
- Do you perceive that love, and not fear, is the ultimate source of evolution for any collective, and feel its correlation with nature, as illustrated by the examples used in this book?
- Do you genuinely crave a world where leaders and ultimately everyone in a collective can always express themselves with truth, and not play politics for personal protection and projection?
- Do you crave to be a part of a culture where the leaders are akin to the conductors in a grand orchestra, in that they lead with trust, not micro-manage the experts within their midst?
- Are you in sync with the need to value the lives of everyone in any collective, and therefore the bravery it takes to seek peace wherever possible?
- Do you feel the strength of a leader who knows what they stand for, and craves destiny for all they lead, even after openly listening to the views of others and valuing their input?

Of course, you may disagree with these perspectives of leadership and that is your undeniable right as a unique individual and my equal in life. I thank you for considering my views about leadership; but you should abide by what you feel is right. I would expect nothing less from anyone than for them to search inside their heart and, once a belief is felt and established, to remain in their full integrity and express that as their truth.

If you agree, however, then please use the following practical exercises to assist you in your journey, and enjoy the following chapters about how to apply evolved leadership qualities to collectives, providing a wider view of what is possible in the cultures we create.

I hope you will come further on this engaging journey into what is truly possible when we open our hearts and minds to a more natural way of being, together. I know we all deserve more, and perhaps it's not the more we have often devoted our energy to in the past!

## 4.20: Practical Aspects of Becoming an Advanced Leader

### The Path Can be a Great Challenge

If the concepts in this book are appealing to you, you may wish to transition to become a more advanced leader yourself. Perhaps you already are one, but your skills could evolve even further. Our evolution is of course unlimited.

From my personal experience, applying the principles in this book are likely to set you apart from other leaders who lead from a place aligned with more traditional paradigms. Undoubtedly, this will show up in the results that you and your team achieve, and others will notice.

You may also feel different, like I did, and question whether you are really fitting into the prevailing leadership culture of your collective. You may also find that your higher integrity feels out of place in a high ego environment, which is less tuned into truth and love.

I would encourage you to persevere in the interests of your own development, though be ever mindful that there may come a time when you feel out of sync with the culture within which you are operating. This may lead you to seriously question whether your future lies comfortably in that collective. Seeking greener pastures and a new flock to shepherd may well become a new and exciting option at some point. This was my personal experience, though may not be possible for you depending on your personal circumstances.

You may also be drawn to become part of a collective where the senior leaders are renowned for leadership that is already highly evolved. This will enable you to grow and hone your skills in a more compatible and supportive environment.

No matter what you choose to do, it is important to recognise that this sort of leadership is not the norm at present, and therefore applying it will not be without its challenges. But imagine a world where this type of leadership catches on and becomes the accepted norm. Wouldn't you love to be at the forefront of this exciting transition?

### Processes to Support Your Advancement

You may be excited to become an advanced leader as described in this book, but not sure where to begin this transformation process. Below is some guidance on this great question.

Initially your transition will be substantially mental. Changing the way you consciously think is a great start. A stronger mind will greatly assist you when embarking on your journey, and facing the changes through which you will ultimately evolve.

Appendix II contains 30 mantras that could be very useful reminders to help you alter your mindset and step into a new beginning. These mantras are also provided on my website at mark-worthington.com as a downloadable printable PDF. You may choose to put this list somewhere accessible, to kick-start your personal transformation.

You may also actively seek to more consciously approach situations as they arise, and challenge yourself to apply the principles you have been drawn to in this book. Indeed, please consider taking this approach before, during and after any leadership experience that you encounter:

### Before the Experience

- Consider how you would seek to lead people through the experience, and what would constitute success to you in your new leadership mindset, other than just particular financial outcomes.

## During the Experience

- Witness how you and others are handling matters and circumstances that arise, and how these could be better dealt with, calling upon your more advanced levels of awareness. For example, has the blame game been in play, or are people becoming competitive in an unhealthy way?
- Remind yourself when you are slipping back into old paradigms of thinking and fitting into norms of behaviour that no longer resonate with your preferred way of leading. This will happen, without doubt, because old habits 'die hard' and conditioning by nature is difficult for the mind to eliminate, because it resides in your mind in the first place. In fact, it's the only place it does live.
- When you catch yourself falling back into old patterns of behaviour don't beat yourself up, just laugh and take the more evolved path from that point on. Self-deprecation will only lower your morale temporarily and detract from your ability to set a positive standard of behaviour for others to follow.

## After the Experience

- This is a great time for self-reflection. In hindsight, how well did you and the team go?
- Give yourself credit for every lift you achieved and celebrate your expansion as a more evolved leader, no matter how small the lift. Remember that no one is perfect, and evolution is never-ending by nature. You will almost certainly get another chance!
- Consider what you would like to apply more comprehensively

next time and take note of any feedback from others, including from learned mentors you may be working with.

However, as well as training yourself consciously and mentally, you will also need to seek deeper self-awareness to support your journey. It is not possible to access this deeper self-awareness, and therefore the true power of your heart or soul, in the mind alone. You will need to really get to know yourself deeply and comprehensively, and this is of course a deliberate choice, and an important one on your journey to making your life, and the lives of others around you, more fulfiling. Appendix I offers you many self-exploration questions to enable you to get to know yourself.

In my book *Where Your Happiness Hides*, and to some extent in this book, I have also spoken of the astonishing power that our unconscious beliefs and past experiences have over the way we live our lives today. In this way, the mind can either hinder or facilitate your transformation journey in a very powerful way. Limiting beliefs can prevent us from truly understanding the depths of ourselves and what we really stand for, and are therefore passionate about. Passion ultimately comes from our heart. We truly can't *think* passion, just like we can't *think* love. Both are a feeling. This is why I often speak of leading with intuition, with love and truth.

The obvious question then becomes *how* do you access and apply these feelings in a world that may not always value them, particularly when they get in the way of achieving short-term or previously accepted goals.

The answer is to 'clear the pipe' that leads you to your heart, then have the courage to listen to its wisdom and live from this place of great poise. This ultimately may mean letting go of the 'previous you', the self your past (and its many experiences) helped to construct. This limited self may be a mere shadow of what you are likely to find when you delve into the depths of yourself.

But beware, this journey is quite addictive! It may show you a brand new true you, further accelerating your evolution as a person and as a leader.

As you get closer to your true self, you may find yourself becoming more present as a person and as a leader, and this will only enhance your transformation. It may also evoke new experiences and feelings that you would like to talk about with someone, in which case please don't hesitate to get in touch. I am happy to assist any readers who are deeply curious at this point.

# CHAPTER 5

# Core Traits of Highly Evolved Collectives

In this chapter we switch from considering the attributes of leaders, to some of the advanced attributes that are highly desirable in evolved collectives. Of course leaders will still be a key determiner of whether those attributes arise and endure in any situation.

## 5.1 Rediscovering the Purity of Life

Our well-being comes from being well. This might sound obvious, but it is a fundamental aspect of life, both individually and collectively, that sometimes gets forgotten.

We often forget to honour our well-being and yet it is our natural state of being. Fundamentally, as individuals, we have an entrenched belief that we deserve to suffer, and that life is therefore hard. Perhaps this arises from our subconscious belief that we will most likely die and be no more. In effect, god or the universe has forsaken us.

Throughout history, religious institutions have taught us that we will get to heaven after we endure a life of sacrifice and devotion. Many seek to retire after an extended period of working for a living, content to wait until their bodies are older before they choose to fully enjoy life. Can you see a tinge of madness in this? Yes, security matters; but in my view we have this out of balance.

So, when you put a collective of individuals together, each of them with this limiting mindset, you simply create the replication of this expectation on a magnified scale. In this place, the collective will always struggle to be well and thrive, for its internal energy will be directed at surviving, not thriving. A sense of obligation, not fun, takes centre stage.

Happiness is the doorway that can open up when we honour and respect our need to be authentic and express ourselves in life. All our choices and priorities can shift, along with our experiences in life when we make conscious decisions about our very existence. And the most dynamic realisation we can come to is that we are here as life first, and everything else will reorganise itself once we become aware of this and live in alignment with it.

When we step back and appreciate that 'we are life', we can lead individuals and collectives from chaos to fluidity, from great harm to health, and from difficulty to well-being. It's just a new belief structure away.

And the basis of this is love, for this is the core essence of our life force and therefore our very existence.

### Well-Being Means Being Well

Most collectives see themselves as having a purpose in what they do, at least in theory. However, in many cases, purpose and well-being are overwhelmed by, and lost in, the desire for financial gain, or the appearance of such 'success'. When we unchain people from the concept of suffering, and replace it with the concept of growing through fulfilling experiences, we open a collective up to pure purpose, through the pure service to all involved, including those inside the collective.

When we are true to life and the well-being of all, there can be pure intention, pure engagement, pure expression, pure outcomes, and pure financial exchanges, because all is based on the premise of purity, and not an inherent expectation of greed overriding all else.

When everyone in a business, or market, or community operate from a place of pure intention, all involved can flourish.

This reference to purity does not mean that everyone involved is perfect or morally superior, it means they are all flowing together in a natural direction that aligns with their hearts. Some might call this love, for they are doing what is natural to them and therefore inspires them.

Picture a river that flows with continuous momentum. The river is cleansed by its natural flow, and because it has a continuous stream of energy. The river is self-cleansing and pure. It moves in the direction intended, for the purpose is intended by nature, and as it does it provides beneficial outcomes for all who rely upon its stream of pure water. If it stagnates, its purity will be lost, and the well-being of those downstream may be diminished, temporarily at least.

The stream of energy that flows through a river can be just like the stream of energy that flows through a collective. When the energy in a collective is natural and pure in its intent, all who participate in that collective will flow as well, in a state of wellness.

In this situation a group of individuals can be well together, and create a dynamic collective. A group of well beings is the end result, you might say.

### Be a Creative, Expressive Organism

We often get caught up in the form, not the substance, of a collective. We think of them as companies, government bodies, partnerships, families, teams, communities, and so on, and our prevailing laws colour our thinking about these bodies.

We all know that a collection of combined cells is known as

an organism. Everything alive on this planet is an organism. Our individual bodies are organisms, comprised of billions of cells.

Leaders who recognise that the collective they lead is an organism, will be well-served. After all, the collection of cells that are human beings come together to create an organ-isation. When this is organised in a natural or organ-ic way, the life-force or creative energy of all those who participate, and who move through its arteries or hallways, can flow together to become creative and expressive in an orgasmic way.

Leaders who understand that they are conducting, or orchestrating, an organism that is alive in the shape of a collective, can release its pure potency for the benefit of all those involved. This advanced awareness is critical to the expression of a paradigm that revels in its own energy, and gathers its own momentum.

When a person, and particularly a leader, accesses the pure energy of love within themselves, they can influence the well-being of all in a continuous flow. Leaders who focus on their own well-being, defined far beyond material gain, can influence the well-being of the collective they lead. This improves the well-being of those they lead, and this then comes back again to their own well-being. It's like a circle, a sphere; and in this sphere, the experience of well-being can become self-generating, for it can be experienced by all. Thus familial leaders who feel and express well-being and contentment help inspire others to pursue the same. It's the same in sporting groups, community activities, schools, colleges, and work places.

Whereas a clear disregard and disrespect for people's well-being in a collective can create great harm, both in its physical and emotional impact on those involved. However, once this cycle is reversed it can become perpetually positive. This is a core role of a leader, even if it is much overlooked from my experience.

All collectives should address the concept of a Wellness Officer in some shape or form, whether it is actually an appointed person, or simply a role someone adopts. Most large business organisations have human resources teams, but they typically represent management, not staff. Most sporting teams have supporters, but they can be just as critical as they can be supportive. Most educational establishments have student counsellors, but they are often in place to protect the school rather than the students themselves. The well-being of others should be a priority and focus.

## The Perception of Success

When leaders become aware that they have the capacity within themselves to live bountiful and abundant lives, irrespective of just money; and when they honour and appreciate the experience of well-being within themselves, they can help to create this same richness of life for all.

As outlined above, much of the commercial and community dysfunction in our world right now can be associated with perceptions of what constitutes 'success'. Most people effectively accept that normal perceptions of 'success' involve metrics related to money.

At an individual level, this might express as the type of home, car, education or holiday you can afford. If those earning the money are stressed and suffering as a result, this is often seen as acceptable trade-offs for the lifestyle achieved.

In a business sense, this might express as financial profits, balance sheets, market shares, dividend levels, and so on. If those working in the business are worn out and unhappy, this may get measured, but is often dismissed as a necessary consequence in the minds of leaders, because they are thinking short-term, and do not draw a line between happiness and financial success.

The same applies to territorial communities, in how we measure the strength of a country – which is usually by financial metrics, or the size or quality of its military power. For example, many countries have traditionally used Gross Domestic Product (GDP) to measure the success of their economies, which has then become a surrogate for measuring success. GDP is effectively a measure of total spending, or income, in an economy.

However, GDP is limited in its ability to measure welfare. It measures the movement of money, but not mental health, cultural resilience, or environmental health. Money does not create happiness beyond a certain level, so therefore GDP is equally limited as a measurement of fulfilment in a nation.

For example, if a person's home is destroyed by a fire or flood and is rebuilt, the cost of the rebuild is counted in GDP figures. However, for the person who lost their home, the spending is not representative of the pain and trauma they would have experienced. And the volume of money was just used to replace an asset that was already functional. The event is therefore of little value to society, other than to lift the flow of money.

The dysfunctions we are currently experiencing as a society partially stem from the fact that we do not honour life enough. We need to define and measure 'success' against different criteria, such as levels of fulfilment, joy, learning, happiness, and financial returns, rather than just the last one.

New Zealand, one of the world's most beautiful countries, introduced a Happiness Index in 2013 to measure the happiness and well-being of its people. Other countries have done the same. Some countries in the world, including Australia, are starting to create 'welfare budgets' to try and measure the impact of money spent on people's happiness and well-being. It is important that money is spent on allowing people to enjoy lives full of purpose, balance and happiness.

In 2022, the UN World Happiness Report listed the top 20 countries in the world for happiness levels. They were, in order:

| 1 | Finland | 11 | Austria |
|---|---|---|---|
| 2 | Denmark | 12 | Australia |
| 3 | Iceland | 13 | Ireland |
| 4 | Switzerland | 14 | Germany |
| 5 | Netherlands | 15 | Canada |
| 6 | Luxembourg | 16 | United States |
| 7 | Sweden | 17 | United Kingdom |
| 8 | Norway | 18 | Czech Republic |
| 9 | Israel | 19 | Belgium |
| 10 | New Zealand | 20 | France |

Interestingly, none of the world's richest nations (like those in the G8) made the top ten. They include: Canada (15th), France (20th), the United Kingdom (17th), Germany (14th), the United States (16th), and Italy, Russia and Japan – which did not make the top 20 at all.

Also interestingly, there is a high proportion of Nordic countries in the top 10 (including Finland, Denmark, Norway, Sweden, and Iceland), with the report concluding that their high scores reflect low levels of corruption, high social trust levels, and elevated levels of freedom, and life expectancy.

What can this data tell us about the role of money in creating happiness and well-being?

Reflecting on my own experiences in some of these countries, I was incredibly impressed with the environmental beauty of Norway, Sweden, Switzerland, Austria, Denmark, and New Zealand. Although I was just a tourist, I felt incredibly relaxed and happy in their natural environments, and this I would contrast to Japan and the United States, where I witnessed great wealth but felt uneasy at times with the congestion in some cities.

One thing I will never forget in Switzerland was seeing shop owners leaving their goods on the street at night, and not locking them up. This baffled me, revealing the country's high levels of social trust.

Here are a few questions we can be asking ourselves about money:

- Why do we have such a focus on money and wealth, if evidence suggests significant wealth may not bring people the happiness they think it will?
- Is our attitude to income and wealth out of step with what we truly desire?
- Are we out of balance on a personal (ie. micro) and collective (ie. macro) basis when it comes to pursuing wealth over well-being?

You be the judge in your own court, then consider applying that judgement in order to honour your own life.

### Honour Your Life As Alive

There is an eternal fountain of life within all of us, which we often fail to recognise. We can learn to appreciate it, however, through the simple acknowledgement that we are each a life-force, having a human experience.

Once we understand this, we can then expose the diminished capacities and concepts by which we currently live. We can instead value our lives, and in turn the lives of others, as an absolute priority; and we can bring forth great purity, intentionality, the energy connected to our hearts, and become represented by a much wiser stream of energy.

When this knowing is felt and understood by a collective, it will unleash energy flows, which reinforce the value of life. In this state, the very experience of living well will become the primary meaning of people's lives. As this re-prioritisation takes place, the existence of the human experience will then shift in an undeniable way.

Nothing exists in our lives without the life force that we inherently are. It is our force, and without it we would be nothing.

Of course, we can never truly be 'nothing' because we are life force living life. Perhaps it's time we recognised this? How often when you are doing something, or leading something, do you stop to value the greatest attribute you possess: that you are alive? Isn't this worth honouring and celebrating?

When you honour the life force that you are, and prioritise that, your life will completely reorganise itself around that which is more valuable to the new you. The energetic pulsations associated with this honouring will be transformative in so many wonderful ways.

I have done this in recent years, as I have re-evaluated what is valuable and interesting enough for me to direct my life force towards. These days, I only focus my energy on the things that add value to my life. In other words, where possible, I try to do what I love and spend time with people I love. This possibility is available to all, although I understand individuals may find it difficult to apply, depending on their circumstances.

Imagine, however, if everyone in a collective could develop this pure authenticity and aliveness? The potency of that collective would shift to an incredible level, as a new set of intentions are formed and aligned, based on the collective understanding that all involved want to honour their life, first and foremost, and are involved because they love the environment within which they live or work. This would amount to inspiration on steroids!

There is nothing (of good intention) that a collective with this level of absolute awareness and aligned intent would not be able to achieve. The possibilities are endless and ever expanding.

## 5.2 Becoming More

The more awareness we have, the more we align our conscious and subconscious minds. In this place we are at one with our feelings and thoughts. We know and align with what we believe in! This is an extremely advanced place to be in, and the closer we get to it, the more potent a leader or an individual in any walk of life can become.

No leader will ever be perfect, but becoming more aware can draw them closer to being an inspiration to others. When a leader has strong self-awareness, and combines this with the right intentions, the sky becomes the limit. After all, intention immediately creates a platform for possibility to emerge; and where our intention goes, energy flows.

Since thoughts manifest as outcomes, the beliefs a leader holds will lead to thoughts, which will result in actions, which will manifest as outcomes. If the beliefs in question are limiting beliefs, they will by definition result in limited outcomes.

The solution to turning this around, can be found in creating more consciousness in the leadership of any group, and have it trickle down to all involved. Herein lies the 'gold' that can enable leaders to shine, and the collectives they represent to thrive.

### Our Natural Desire for More

Nothing stands still. The universe is constantly expanding and all within it follows suit. It's a rhythmic but slow process. It's unstoppable. It's natural for all organisms on Earth to expand or evolve.

Humans naturally crave more. We want, and sometimes, demand more. Societies hope to have more, scientists are continually explaining more, and nations compete for more. This is a primal instinct in all of us. Few want to stand still (unless it's scary to move).

But what is the 'more' in question? Our society speaks of having more, achieving more, finding more, or making more. But rarely does it speak of *becoming* more.

Our definition of 'more' has become habitually defined by a series of narrow external concepts related to money and power, not things that really matter to our hearts, like expansion and joy. We are very outcome-focused in all walks of life, and this can limit our potential over the longer term to achieve the 'more' that is truly possible, and which our hearts desire. The more it desires comes from the inside, expanding outwards, not from the outside expanding inwards. It is a feeling, not a thing. It matters, but it's not matter.

A collective will often measure it's success by concepts (often monetary ones such as financial profits, market share, share price, and so on), and these measures can be important; but, in the same way that profit must be balanced against purpose, people and the planet, these measures are just part of the story.

There is a fundamental difference between expansion and inflation. When an individual or collective needs inflation it fundamentally needs more of something to feel secure and properly valued. There is a strong link here to fear. Inflation can become insatiable when it stems from a need for more.

Think of inflation in an economy. When inflation exceeds income growth, it means more money is required to maintain the lifestyles of those involved, because their money buys them less. Minor amounts of inflation are considered acceptable. Where it results from an expanding economy or growing population, it can bring benefits to those involved. However, devoid of expansion and real productivity gains, inflation is a limiting place to be and damaging for any economy or collective. It truly gives us the wrong more!

For any collective to flourish, their advancement needs to be based on true expansion and growth. And this expansion is best achieved internally within a collective, before it can manifest more externally on a sustainable level.

Human beings in their hearts are all fundamentally seeking to feel fulfilled, loved and happy. They seek to experience life in an authentic way as their true selves. Many, however, are just not aware of this in their minds. It lurks within their very being, and can be subconscious for many.

Organisations, societies, and nations are all fundamentally the same because they are comprised of people conditioned in similar ways. Great leadership can, however, make a huge difference to unlocking this conditioning, or at least defusing it. To do this, they must start by becoming aware of the desire for and sense of expansion within themselves, and then within their collective. Are they leading the collective for inflation only, or are they determined to create an environment in which all involved can flourish, create, and fulfil themselves through personal expansion?

When a leader of a collective and its constituents expand or grow their ability to be more, through continuous expansion, they will enhance their ability to include more in all that takes place. In this place of openness and freshness, inclusiveness can breed a feeling of further inclusiveness, which all involved will sense. All can become more and create more.

The more inclusive any environment becomes, the more can flourish – the diversity of relationships, creative ideas and desires.

Inclusion, not exclusion, is the gateway to exponential change, for it supports expansion for all, rather than inflation for the few.

## 5.3 The Forgotten Power of the Sphere

Our world, and the universe within which we exist, is based on the shape of spheres. The Earth, our moon, the planets, and the sun are all spheres, and they move around each other in spherical orbits. Everything in Earth's system can be placed into one of four major subsystems – land, water, living things and air – and these four subsystems are all classified as spheres. Scientists call them the litho*sphere* (land), hydro*sphere* (water), bio*sphere* (living things), and the atmo*sphere* (air). Each of these spheres can then be further divided into sub-spheres. They all keep us alive in some way. Our journey into life even commences inside a fertilised egg or sphere, and we grow from there. Sacred geometry depicts how all living things emanate from a sphere and grow.

The advantage of a sphere is that it supports movement and freedom. The wheel itself has allowed humans to travel more easily across the land.

In contrast to this, squares, pyramids, and rectangles struggle to promote movement.

The sphere is a source of fluidity and a symbol of possibility in our lives. Picture the Olympic symbol and what it stands for: the pinnacle of sporting success.

Our world is also based on atoms, which are comprised of spherical electrons that orbit around each other, like so in this simplistic depiction:

Figure 3: The Spherical Anatomy of an Atom

We cannot escape from spheres. They surround us, keep us alive, and are what we are made from. Our lives are even constantly evolving, just like our Earth is constantly spinning and moving around the sun. We never truly stop moving, though, in many ways, we have moved away from this way of being in our minds. We resist change and fear, going anywhere but straight up – to what we perceive to be the top of a pyramid.

Indeed, much of our society has become structured around linear shapes that reflect our traditional obsession with hierarchy and relative importance. Central business districts are often characterised by skyscrapers and towers, rectangles reflecting the relative importance of those businesses. Senior executives get the views from the top floors, while mailroom staff reside in the basement. In residential apartment blocks, the supposed 'best' is the penthouse at the top.

Similarly lineal dynamics within a collective, such as a pyramid, can influence its focus as outcome-based, because they determine the flow of energy within a collective. However, where the dynamics and capacities of a collective and the individuals involved are in the shape of a sphere, that collective is constantly capable of expanding, recharging, reinspiring, and feeding itself, because energies, intellects and creativity come into greater fluidity and equality.

Take your typical large business organisation as an example. It typically looks like this internally:

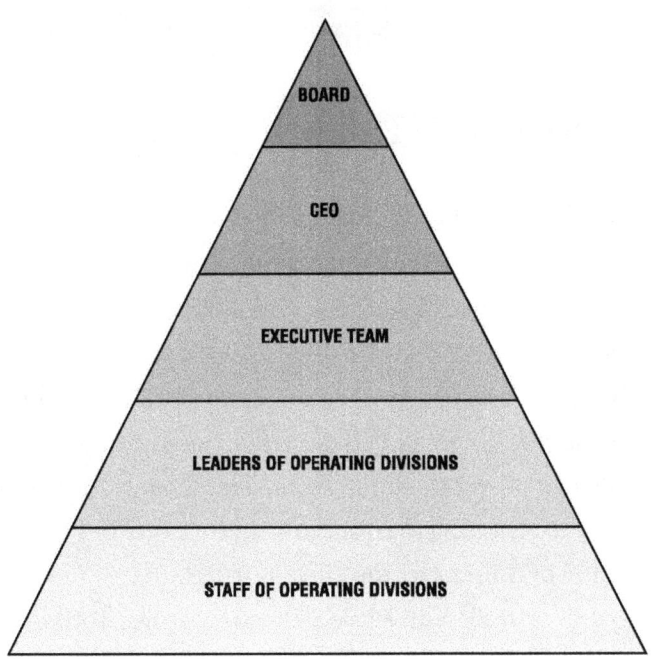

Figure 4: The Normal Business Pyramid of Power

Wouldn't it be better if it looked and operated like this instead?

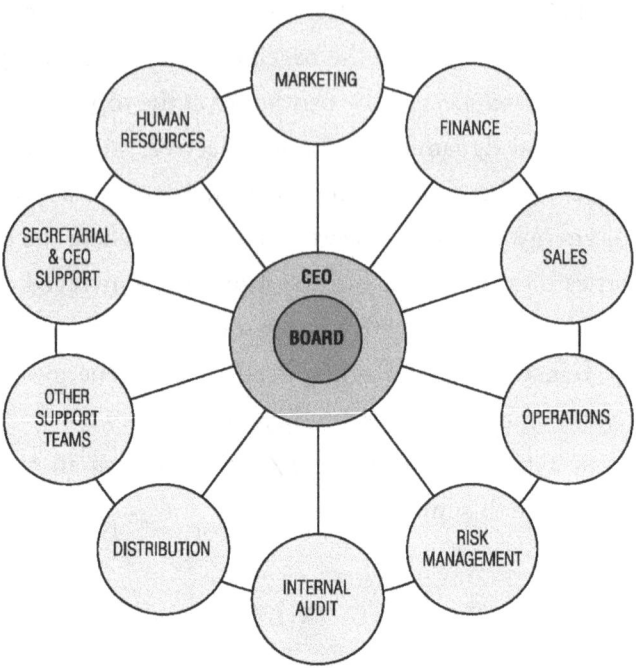

Figure 5: The Flexible Sphere of Business

When all parts of a collective have equal access to their leader, and equal opportunity to contribute ideas and views, a collective can be in greater balance, and can expand as it continues to grow.

Of course, in larger collectives this concept can be more challenging to apply, but the principles are the same. At different points, various parts of the sphere, such as different divisions, could perhaps have greater influence on proceedings as needed. This would be akin to a particular musician taking the lead for a short period in a musical score, at the direction of the conductor.

However it is resolved, every collective grows through its own awareness, and that awareness is best generated from within a sphere, not just from the top. To do otherwise is to put a limit on possibility.

When we can move away from a linear or hierarchical mindset, which is predicated on energy primarily flowing in one direction, we can escape from our rigid constructs. As we do this, our collectives can become more inclusive, as can the designs of our cities and places of work. Spheres and circles allow inclusion and expansion. In this way, they can create more through the subtle power of equality. They allow continuous refreshment to take place as individuals collaborate to cocreate.

Evolved collectives see the world as spherical, for this is nature expressing itself naturally.

## Returning to the Round Table Concept

Most contemporary boardroom and executive tables are rectangular in shape. The chairperson usually sits in the same place at each meeting, and the more important you are, the closer you sit to the chairperson. Any new member or visitor usually sits at the extremities of the table, commensurate with their perceived level of importance.

Compare this to the famous round table of King Arthur legend. Arthur and his knights congregated around the table, and as such all had equal positioning. The round table concept implied that all who sat around that table had equal opportunity to contribute to the discussion.

No one knows if this round table truly existed, or was just a tale, but the principles it stood for have been watered down with our modern mindsets of hierarchy and the commonly applied linear flow of insights and decisions. Of course King Arthur, in his court, still made decisions, but he did so after receiving the creative input and views of all present, and who wanted to have their say.

The round table concept is not new; it has been around for hundreds of years. However, many collectives seem to have forgotten its value in our modern world. Even if there is a physical round table, its intent can be easily overridden by the command-and-control style of the leaders, such that it may as well have been rectangular.

## Expansion is Natural, Not Normal

Our universe is constantly expanding and, as such, it never goes back to where it was before. It can't.

The universe evolves, and so must we, individually and collectively. This is truly unstoppable, irrespective of what we might think. Anything that stops this natural flow of evolution will eventually be replaced, for it must. Nature wins out in the end.

But instead of acknowledging this expansive state, we have become obsessed with principles of 'higher' and 'lower' (a limiting concept), separation and segregation (an impossible concept), and inflation and deflation (a narrow concept). In all this subconscious interplay, equality has been lost, and the principle of expansion has become meaningless, not meaningful. We seek to become higher, not more expansive. Inflation has replaced expansion; and inflation is not a meaningful representation of more – it requires more, but it's not intrinsically a representation of more.

Meaningful evolution must instead come from embracing our ever-expanding spheres of influence, and tapping into inspirations that arise within us all, should we choose to listen. Squares, triangles, and rectangles by their very nature are not fluid; they keep us disconnected from each other and the potency that can flow from equality in motion.

Evolved collectives are transparent spheres, fully charged and creating endless possibilities, and they acknowledge their scope for true expansion.

## Communicating Through the Sphere

The shape of a sphere in collectives allows information and ideas to easily flow in different directions, and without being blocked or trapped by corners of control. It can exist when the right mindsets support it.

The pyramid structure when applied to people implies one person is more important than others. It promotes rigidity, blocks creativity, instils fear, and creates situations in which communication is sent down from above to those of a perceived lesser standing.

Such arrangements take people away from their freedom to express what they believe. It creates 'yes' people, who tend to adopt the stated communications from above as truth or 'gospel', and who therefore stop contributing their own creative ideas to a situation or challenging the status quo. And why would they contribute when the structure, and the means of communication in a collective, do not promote or encourage upward feedback?

Those at the top of a pyramid also receive different subliminal messages from their lofty position at the top: that they are more important and matter more to the collective than those at their base.

The ancient Egyptians, and several other ancient civilisations, used the pyramid shape to create structures because they believed that it helped them to communicate with the divine. They believed that this provided access to higher powers in the sky. Pyramids were also considered to be highly structurally functional, being powerful in their resistance to the elements, including flood and earthquakes. These ancient people probably knew more than we give them credit for.

Pyramids do have their place for some practical reasons. Under our current laws, group structures of companies often take such a shape with holding companies owning other group entities. Superimposing the pyramid structure over the spherical management, or people structure, creates the following guiding vision of how a larger collectives could look conceptually, to give it fluidity, creativity, and functionality to meet legal requirements:

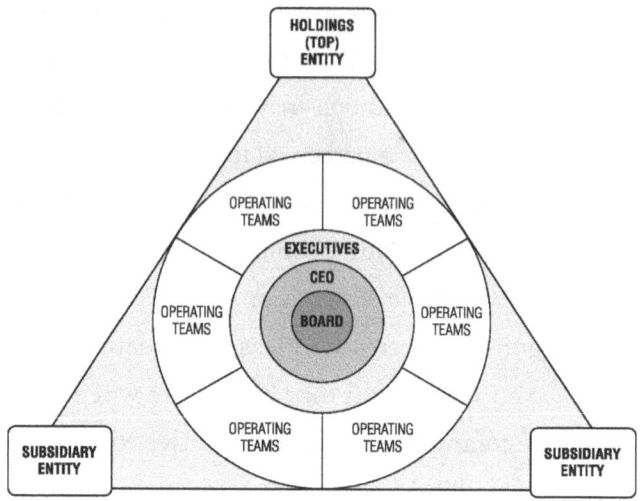

Figure 6: The Fluid Sphere Within the Pyramid

However, pyramid structures could also be inverted and overlaid, as in the diagram below, including a sphere at its centre:

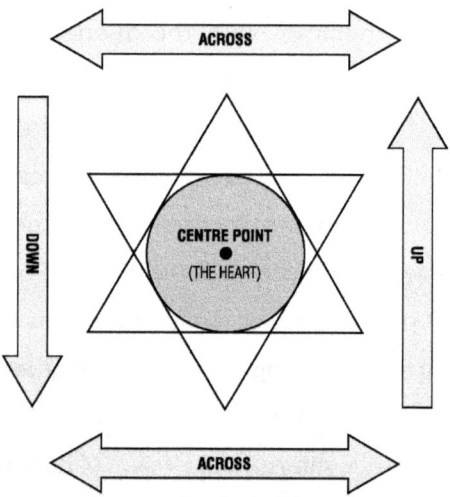

Figure 7: The Energy Flows Possible Within the Inverted Pyramid

This structure could still service the flow of key decisions downward, but with an inverted pyramid it could also allow the flow of energy and ideas upward, and to some extent across the organisation. This would take account of the fact that everyone in a collective is valued and intelligent.

### The Sphere Within the Sphere

The whole structure could also become a sphere, with separate smaller spheres orbiting the central sphere, while still contained within the whole sphere or universe of the collective.

What if it looked like this?

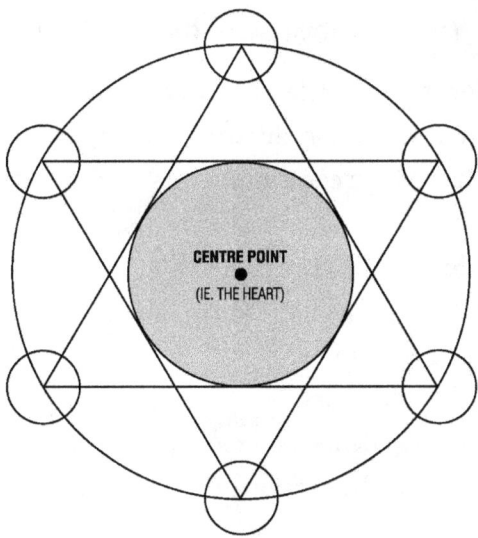

Figure 8: The Sphere Within the Sphere

This outer sphere could place the whole structure into a greater place of fluidity and balance, removing any rough edges, which otherwise limit the collective from expanding as it grows and learns. This could be a pathway to connecting energy within the whole structure and allowing flow in a number of directions.

The ancient Egyptians understood the power of this shape, as can be seen in their symbolisms and hieroglyphics. The Jewish flag includes the Star of David. Spiritual people also hold it dear as the 'chariot' to the afterlife, known as the Merkabah. It is seen as our door to the divine by many. It is a natural shape we have largely missed in our modern world, as we have rushed to take power over each other.

Some at the top probably subconsciously prefer pyramids and rectangular shapes, because it is these shapes that give them privileges, which they may have worked hard to enjoy or inherit from others. That's not a criticism, as these beliefs spring from our conditioned minds. Climbing the ladder of success is a much-used expression. But who do we climb over and look down upon to get there?

## The Possibilities of the Six Points

The six points, or smaller circles, in my depiction above, are significant because they can stand for differing principles or pillars of any collective, which can then contribute to its success, such as:

1. Purpose through wisdom
2. Creating through the right work
3. Investing for the future
4. Complying with the law
5. Not being solely defined by money
6. Supporting those less fortunate

The Jewish religion teaches these principles, and they are revered for their prowess with money!

A number of these have been touched on above, so I will be brief in describing them.

### *1. Purpose Through Wisdom*

We are all creative when we can find the space to access our intuition. It's here that great wisdom can be accessed.

When we use wisdom to paint the purpose and direction of a

collective, we can direct our energies to where they should naturally flow.

If making money alone is our purpose, the game of success is hard to sustain. We truly cannot pursue money without attaining wisdom first. Wisdom creates money, money does not create wisdom. Expansion of our self-awareness is a great contributor to higher levels of wisdom. They are closely linked.

## 2. Creating Through the Right Work

Human beings are creative more than anything else. We deeply seek to create.

However, have we become consumers obsessed with receiving, rather than creators who are here to give and receive in equal measure? If so, how did we learn this way of being?

Elevated levels of productive work are important in any collective. However, if people get 'flogged' or sacrificed just to create financial outcomes, if they get stressed and stop enjoying life, then short-term financial profit motives can eclipse all else, and therefore sustainable returns on effort. They may even fail before they succeed.

However, wisdom combined with logic and creativity has great potential to result in a positive outcome for us all.

## 3. Investing for the future

All collectives must be inherently sustainable. Short-term thinking can create atrophy if sustainability is ignored. Once the herd has eaten all the sustenance in the field it is in, it needs to know where it is going next.

There are countless stories of once-great collectives dominating their industries, only to fail because they did not look ahead to anticipate the future. Names that come to mind include Kodak, Polaroid, and Compaq.

Collectives, to be sustainable, must invest in their futures sufficiently, and to do this they need to retain and actively apply financial profits capable of funding this on a regular basis. Families need to invest in their future togetherness. Colleges need to invest in providing students with memorable experiences to encourage alumni relationships. Businesses need to invest in good customer service to encourage consumer loyalty.

The future will not take care of itself.

### 4. Complying with the law

To be successful, any individual or collective needs to comply with the law. The law is there for a reason, and normally has a sound basis to create harmony in collectives.

By the same token, laws need to be sensible and respect the rights of people. Authority without compassion must be challenged by the people it is meant to serve!

We were not born to serve governments. It truly is the other way around.

### 5. Not being solely defined by money

Money is important. We all need it to give us the energy of life. Without it, we will not be abundant in life. It allows us to grow in our current world.

However, when it is seen as our principal reason for work, balance and fulfilment can be lost. Our attachment to money is a problem in the modern world, and it is based on a fear that we need to compete for resources to be valuable.

Of course we are all worthy, regardless of our level of wealth. Money is a blessing, but on its own can be soulless – unless it is used to create a better life, full of love and the expansion of awareness.

We need to own money. It should not own us.

A balanced collective understands this and has a sense of where money sits on its priority list. We must always be conscious of the 4 Ps.

### 6. Supporting those less fortunate

We must all give and receive in equal measure. To some extent, our world has lost sight of this, and many individuals and collectives seek to only receive, or to give in anticipation of a pay back. They do not give out of care or integrity; they give for inflation or image creation.

Money should travel around our economies in a circular flow, much like the outer circle of our new sphere. But this circular flow can be distorted by greed, unfair or unwise government rules, and the need for more wealth.

All our energy needs to be in motion, and it will flow with greater power when it comes from the e-motion of love. Here it can be in alignment with the natural order of expansion and the universe.

## Creating the Current of Currency

When a collective and its leaders are aligned with what is of interest or value to the collective's purpose, they can, and will, find the true value of their money's expression. The current of money will flow towards their intention, which will be pure in its nature. This kind of currency truly has its own current because a noble enterprise with honourable intentions and a heart, will be supported by its market.

Many people in commercial and corporate collectives, including its leaders, are too focused on what they can gain for themselves through operating the business, and making money. Much energy is devoted to making money, counting it, and spending it. Much effort is therefore spent without any true value or reference to the common good.

Individuals can also exhibit similar tendencies, with self-interest driving most of us to focus primarily on our own financial well-being.

An advanced leader understands the value of resources that flows through their position, and what they can do with it to create a vastly different environment for all concerned, especially those they lead. The challenge is to stop merely managing the numbers, and instead recognise their ability to influence the continued expansion of resources.

The word resource says so much that we miss. Money is a source of energy that is constantly on offer. When purpose, interest, and value are aligned with positive, valuable intent, money inflows will repeat when the right energies are applied. Sure, money can be made from manipulation or subconscious means, but this has a limited 'shelf life', as society will not resource this type of intention forever. Karma comes!

The expansion of a collective's resources will flow with abundance once it can see that money needs to flow through it in order to energise a positive intention. It is not truly the end outcome for money to be hoarded and idolised, as is currently the norm.

That doesn't mean you can't own money and buy a beautiful home by the sea. If this serves a wonderful purpose to benefit you or your family, why not have it? After all such an intention is based on love – the love of one's family. Love is the cornerstone of life. Its sphere of influence is unlimited. We've just forgotten that perhaps.

## 5.4 Redefining the Concepts of Winning and Losing

While many of us do extraordinary things in order 'to win', most of us simply try to win by not losing.

But what if there were no winning or losing? What if we were to move away from conditioned definitions of success – like money, status, and power – and replace them with different concepts like fulfilment, happiness, and expansion? The idea of winning and losing wouldn't be so simple to define.

Things can, and will, go seemingly 'wrong' in life, no matter what you seek to achieve. I say seemingly because there is always a different way of looking at things. Life is constantly giving us challenges and less than ideal outcomes. If we lack the awareness to see these as experiences from which we can grow, then we remain stuck in the winner/loser mindset, and this can be highly destructive to individuals and collectives alike.

Evolved collectives and their individuals are able to identify this as a consequence of a conditioned mind, and align themselves with the universal principle that all is constantly expanding. We are a part of nature, and therefore by definition we must evolve and change. In the long run we can't stop this from taking place (although many try out of ignorance or fear), so it is better to simply embrace change and surrender to expansion, and even better to try to enjoy the process. I now find it awesome and extremely rich in personal fulfilment. After all, how can we grow our awareness, and understand our true capabilities, if we refuse to deeply embrace them and remove the obstacles that stand in their way of expression?

Rita Mae Brown in 1983 famously defined insanity as:

> "Doing the same thing over and over again and expecting different results."

To get better, therefore, of course we have to do something different. If all we do is stay safe and secure, our many possibilities are unlikely to be sparked into reality.

The philosopher Buckminster Fuller once said:

> "We are all called to be architects of the future, not its victims."

If we want to create something of beauty, we are likely to experience setbacks along the way. You can't create a rainbow without rain, or a beach without erosion. Expansion sometimes requires mishap. But these mishaps are the raindrops enabling rainbows to form and glow.

Others' definitions of success are truly irrelevant if you know in your heart what you want to be or do. You own your life, no one else does. Here lies true freedom!

The world rewards innovation, and creative endeavours that make the world a better place.

Think of Apple and the smartphone. It changed all our lives in so many ways, and it started out as just a dream.

## A Cultural Case Study: Apple

One of the largest business organisations in the world is Apple. Its success has been phenomenal, with its market capitalisation bigger than some countries. Its products have quite literally changed the world, particularly the iPhone, iPad, and Apple Watch. Why has Apple been so successful? Because its products are tremendously sought after by customers, being easy-to-use and merging multiple devices into one.

But the work culture at Apple has also stood them apart. It is regarded as extremely positive, in alignment with the company's values, and conducive to great outcomes. According to a 2022 report by Grove, a US consulting organisation, they stand for:

- Creativity and innovation – the company loves to break normal standards and encourages employees to come up with new ideas way outside the box.
- Moderate competition – Apple encourages collaboration and teamwork and is intolerant of excessive internal competition.
- Excellence – the company promotes excellence in its workforce and strives to hire only outstanding talent.
- Teamwork – Apple believes in the power of teamwork and avoids internal bureaucracy by avoiding committee activities. Staff are encouraged to trust each other, and Apple is famous for functioning on ideas, not hierarchy.
- Integrity – Apple expects integrity, including secrecy, for this prevents ground-breaking innovation from leaking to competitors.

Apple is therefore seen by many as having an inspiring culture.

If you have ever been in an Apple store, and bought one of their products or returned one, you can feel the energy that their people and premises project. It is fun and uplifting, and full of trust in customers.

The market capitalisation of Apple reflects the amazing fact that this company really has found a wonderful recipe for success. I recognise that this is only a financial measure, but its growth in profits is obviously a sign of massive consumer demand for their products. Apple has defined its values and, from all accounts, this seems to bring them to life for the good of all. Interestingly, its head office is also the shape of a sphere. Its ability to expand in the future may be limitless, even though its current value is clearly extraordinary.

Other leaders, who can find this level of wisdom within themselves, can help to take other collectives on this same kind of amazing journey. In my career I was sometimes criticised for spending more money than average on staff training and well-being. However, I had discovered the link between these areas and staff retention and productivity, and I received the benefits as a leader, as did the organisations that I worked for. It's not complicated! Value comes back from those you value.

### Legal Structures Redefined

Apple is a clear example of creative expansion generating corporate growth based on the idea that people matter more than structures. Legal structures have, in particular, become overly prevalent in much of our lives. To some extent, legalities have become even more real and important to our leaders than people, because they are tools in the game of making money.

Indeed, we live within a litigious myriad of entities, constructed by the human mind to assist in the determination and protection of financial gain. We are thus buried in a sea of companies, trusts, partnerships, non-profit organisations, charities, religious organisations, and even governments, all of which we often perceive as equal or more important than people. Leaders strive to make these collectives successful because this is where their 'bread is buttered' so to speak. The cost and effort that goes into maintaining these structures is often significant, because many of them have been dreamt up by humans for financial protection or taxation purposes, and in the process, they make many lawyers very rich.

However, we have become lost in this constructed world of legal entities. Everything – when you boil it down – should be owned or created for the benefit of people. The reality is that these mind-created entities don't have feelings or intelligence. They don't have a spirit. If these elements are present in a collective, they are present through the collective beliefs and interactions of its stakeholders, not the fictitious structure registered with the government.

This whole situation has become out of balance, such that we now subrogate our lives to legal structures and government decisions.

It's time we served our fellow humans, not legal constructs without feelings. We can talk about the culture or spirit of a collective, but the reality is that intrinsic energy is derived from the people within it; not the legal structure that our laws establish or the computers it runs on. Advanced leaders see this illusion for what it really is and care for people in a balanced way.

In the end we all came to Earth to live our lives, not meet the endless rules derived from governments.

## Discovering Real Wealth

If you breakdown the word 'wealth' you can derive the concepts of 'well' and health'. Real wealth in any collective is measured by the health and well-being of its members. Money helps, but it certainly can't achieve all that we need to be truly 'wealthy'. If you are having fun, learning, and turning whatever you see as interesting and valuable into meaningful contributions to the world, is that not better than just making money and/or receiving recognition? Who is the 'winner' here?

Many collectives try to beat any opposition they might have to become 'number one' in their area. But this puts a false ceiling on possible levels of success. What if everyone just strived for excellence in all they did and spent less energy on competing to win over others. If the product or service a person produces is as 'perfect' as possible, and it's well-priced, surely they will reap great benefits, as will their customers.

Is our obsession with competing, winning, and not losing, limiting our ability to be the best we can be and to bring forth new possibilities? The more we focus on what others are doing, the more we can be deflected away from the magic that our inner world could help us imagine and build. Be inspired and in admiration of the extraordinary feats of others, then do you as well as *you* can!

## The Organisation of Our Hearts' Desires

I have worked for many large and highly respected organisations. They were all financially successful (when measured against typical business priorities such as financial profits, share price and market share), they paid their taxes, their staff worked hard and were well-paid, and their accomplished executives performed at elevated levels with great commitment. By normal standards, many of these leaders had elite business minds and capacities. Much of this is normal in the 'top end of town', where I worked for many years.

But such businesses could be so much more if their leaders understood the power of a collective of happy people and struck up the harmonies needed to open up possibilities and maximise their potential. The core contributor to these harmonies in any collective, and to the fluidity of creative power, is the self-awareness of the leaders. This allows every member of the collective to express their uniqueness in a united way.

Whether we are at work or at play, our deepest desires to expand – in all we do – comes from first understanding what we love to do.

Our desire to grow as a person does not profoundly change at its core, whether we are in our roles inside a family, business, society or alone with ourselves. We all want to be deeper in our hearts and grow, while interacting with each other in a connected way, for here love is present.

Thus the greatest piece of advice anyone could give anyone in life is: to do and be what you love. In this place, passion and positive emotion is possible, and if you have the courage to step into this, the sky is the limit. This is the true version of winning.

## Resistance Can Create Great Suffering

People dislike and resist change, because in our minds it exposes us to risks and potential downsides that might devalue us. But what about the potential upsides? And isn't this resistance contrary to our inherent desire to be more and to learn from experiences?

Everything in life comes with both a rip-off and a pay-off. In other words, no matter whether we stay still or advance, there will always be positive and negative aspects present. But the payoffs are likely to be much greater if we step into new possibilities aligned with love.

Sometimes our sight can only see the bad and not the good, because we look at the world through a lens of fear when contemplating change. Our lives are predicated on a desire to stay safe. However, on very many occasions, staying still can be far more dangerous than changing, for we will miss the many opportunities that surround us. It is all dependent upon your perspective, and this is where foresight needs to combine with insight. Looking inward and outward both have great (but different) powers.

For example, waves in a storm can be seen as both dangerous and beautiful, depending on your perspective. If you are watching from a hilltop, they can be exhilarating. If you are in a boat or canoe out at sea, they can be terrifying. You cannot say every wave in a storm is bad. Some waves can refresh and invigorate, giving new and exciting opportunities to expand and grow. It is all a matter of perspective, and your willingness to throw yourself against the waves of life.

When a collective stagnates, or is less successful than it aspires to be, it can react with positive energy to the waves it encounters, or it can take a victim position and allow itself to be stuck in a state of stagnation. When powerful waves strike, and we are in the wrong position, we need to move with the new world, or paradigm, and realign ourselves.

Resistance to change can lead to a major source of suffering, for it can merely prolong our exposure to pain and disappointment, particularly in times of great dysfunction. Resistance stops new experiences and learnings form being possible and becoming great sources of new wisdom. So letting go of suffering as a concept is a great way for individuals and collectives to operate.

Advanced leaders with high self-awareness are wise enough to re-evaluate current circumstances as they alter and move their people with any shifts in the ecosystem they collectively inhabit. They act like a shepherd moving their flock to more advantageous pasture. The best leaders inspire their flocks with the insights and foresights they possess and bring them to bear when they are most needed. They create environments that are fluid, and not mired in resistance and the fear of change! In fact when disruption takes centre stage they will dream of transformation, not just incremental change.

### The Link Between Fear, Need, and 'Death'

The human ego is a great creator of fear. It witnesses life, and with great logic works out what we need to feel validated, safe, and successful. This logic, however, can lead us away from our heart's desires or love, because it is based primarily in thought and need.

Once we fear something, our minds can cleverly create a need for that fear. Needs and fears are thus closely aligned. If we fear not getting something, we go in search of that thing or experience to quell the ego's constant reminder that without it we are lesser, effectively taking a chunk out of our self-esteem. The self-perceptions that lurk in our minds, of what we must do or achieve, then allow that created need to take us out of presence, rather than into the richness of our own awareness.

My father always used to say to me when I was growing up, "come-on, it won't kill you", when referring to something I feared. This would have been great advice had I been fully open to hearing it. I know he was trying to teach me to be brave, but often my mind had other ideas.

Leaders need to understand that fears and needs can be highly damaging to a collective and its individuals if they are not brought to the surface and directly addressed. When people's fears are not faced, they can destroy self-esteem as they align with our modern version of death – the death of our own expectations and image points.

In a collective there is a myriad of egos, all seeking similar or different sources of validation. A nation or society can be comprised of millions of people with such varying fears.

Some fears are more common than others, with the most common fears lying in image – including looks, financial status, sexual perception, seniority, levels of power, and our perceived failures or successes. The greatest fears are of course our need to survive, our need for money to value ourselves, and our need for sexual interaction to fulfil our need for procreation. Of course we truly don't need excess levels of money to be genuinely happy, and procreation is truly optional in our modern world. Still, in a collective, the traumas that centre around money and relationships can be exaggerated beyond measure.

This is where an evolved leader can make all the difference. When a leader is deeply centred in themselves, and can eliminate their core fears, neediness diminishes, and inappropriate behaviours (that can energetically harm us, such as elevated levels of excess competition) can be tempered. Great leaders know this, and so immediately address any fears that can be dealt with, both within themselves and within their collective, helping to create a higher sense of self-esteem for all. Unity of thought becomes a common bond.

To do this, they must first find the centre of themselves, or at least be expanding towards their own true sense of self. This allows others to witness what that looks like, and how it can change a person's ability to handle disappointments and challenges. When they are on this path, evolved leaders can show others how to be more present in their personal lives and work endeavours, and create an absence of fear (or at least its diminution in a collective), so the energy of love can step forward to drive creation. This can and will create greater harmony, because neediness, anxieties and egoic driven self-interest levels can all be reduced.

To lead in this way takes courage and vulnerability, for it means stepping into your own feelings and confronting your own fears, and related bouts of neediness, so you can role model what others will benefit from seeing. Evolved leaders need to be like the tin man in The Wizard of Oz and take the journey to find their own heart. Once the leader finds their heart, others in the collective will believe they have a licence to do the same.

Younger generations, and those with higher consciousness, are beginning to demand a higher standard of presence and authenticity from the collectives within which they work, live and play; as well as the leaders who guide them. They are less conditioned than previous generations, for they dare to consider the possibilities of new paradigms. They dare to dream beyond security.

They know there is a more authentic way to be, though they may not know what that way of being is – yet!

Higher awareness, combined with real life experience, can lead these open-hearted members of a collective into an exciting future, where great freedom and fluidity are fully present for all to enjoy.

## 5.5 The Need for Better Questions

The importance of questions is vastly underrated, in all levels of society. In many ways they are more fundamental than the answers they inspire. Questions are drivers of answers and can ultimately lead to the creation of higher awareness, for they stem from a quest for greater awareness. Sharp enquiry can lead to sharp answers, which can cut through to new levels of awareness. They are like a scalpel in the hands of a highly skilled surgeon. Their incisions team-up with nature to create desired outcomes. They speed up the power of healing and enhancement.

Questions, however, must be accompanied by the process of listening, so that they become capable of inspiring great connections with others, and with our own awareness. The higher our intelligence and level of self-awareness, the higher the quality of the questions that we ask. In turn, this influences the intelligence levels embedded in the answers we achieve, the strength of our possibilities and opportunities, and how in turn we can expand. It is an amazing cycle of growth, leading to the possibility of more growth.

A constant stream of intelligent questions, once met by intelligent answers, can then create highly efficient and energised collectives – the kind we all desire, even if we don't realise yet what's possible. It's an exciting prospect for us all, and one I can highly recommend from my personal experience, although it takes patience and commitment!

### Questioning Our Questions

Many of the questions currently being asked are leading us into unhealthy and unnatural outcomes that merely lead us to incremental achievements, at best, and a repeat of known understandings. They are aligned with old paradigms that are due for a rethink. Many of these old questions are fundamentally incapable of creating what we as collectives desire – a paradigm shift to a whole new level.

As an example, if we just keep asking 'how do I own more, or own more than others' what impact do you think that has on our lives? What if we asked, "how can we all be more"?

Our questions can be more intelligent, more creative. Our questions can be of a purer intent.

## Our Big Blind Spot

One of humanity's biggest blunders is not being able to see that we are part of creation itself. We believe that we are somehow distinct from the universal power of creation, and this fundamental misalignment places us as primarily consumers. Humans are unequivocally the key creative force in our world. Technology and progress are not the creators. We are, because we build the technology and instigate the progress. We are not separate from universal energies, we *are* it.

So, if we are part of creation, and not innocent by-standers, what kind of questions should we be asking ourselves and others? What do we ask creation itself, when we realise that we are creation?

Right now, people are arguably asking the wrong questions of businesses, societies, communities, and governments. To change our perspectives and enhance our ability to become the creators we already are, we must ask our questions from a higher place of consciousness, which we all truly already are.

Our current mindsets are focused on certainty, not creativity. As a race we struggle to tolerate uncertainty, because of our need for security. It is no one's fault. It has become a habit on a mass scale and a product of our immersion in human history. Our minds create plans based on what they can perceive has occurred previously, which serves as a blueprint for the next generation. We subconsciously learn in our childhoods that we're judged harshly if we show too much creativity or question authority. It's a sad road to inauthenticity. True selves are lost on this journey, and no one really wins.

But this process blocks what is possible in our present moment, and limits our capacity to expand and find out what is truly possible. Fear, as it always does, holds us back from the something we genuinely want.

Our obsession with certainty strangles innovation. It inhibits exploration and promotes stock-standard expressions. And stock-standard expressions lead to stock-standard outcomes. We get locked into incremental change, and not the transformation we truly desire.

Better questions can aid and abet our attempts to escape this cycle.

### Asking Questions of Our Fears

Much has been written about fear by scholars and spiritually respected masters and authors. We all know that fear is the flip side of love, but that love conquers fear.

But all great philosophy and theory aside, how can we actually remove the fear that is deeply embedded in most of us, and how can we become brave enough to escape the neediness that challenges us?

The first step is to acknowledge that our minds are smart enough to know what will threaten our survival, and adroitly steer us in a different direction. We can trust them to do this, as much of this is instinctual.

If our minds truly think that our survival is at stake, they will drive us to take action. Anything more than this is questionable, and can be questioned, if we so choose. Thus we will avoid the bear in the woods. We will make money to pay for food, safety and shelter. But then we must ask ourselves: are we being driven to make more money than we truly need to be happy and content? Or are we trying to satisfy preconditioned notions of image and success? Even though our minds are ours, they can be hard to control, particularly our subconscious minds, which so strongly influence the decisions we make.

Fear is an indicator of something we think we need to address, such as a belief or influence. We cannot simply tell fear to go away, or tell ourselves that the fear does not exist; we must instead confront the underlying reason for its existence. We must understand that our mind has created the fear for a purpose. In this way it is our friend or ally, and if we engage with it with love, by asking about its true intent, it can teach us much.

When I was younger, I watched the famous shark movie *Jaws*. After seeing the movie, I was terrified of swimming or surfing in the ocean for years. Even though I knew that the odds of being attacked by a shark were minuscule, my subconscious mind remembered that movie all too well. This is a by-product of living in our egos, and not having a sufficient level of awareness of the beliefs that direct our lives. Limited self-awareness leads to limited thinking. But when we investigate our fears, our egos can give way to a more balanced way of thinking, which can allow more spontaneity into our lives.

Some fears, once investigated, may even seem sensible and therefore worth hanging onto. There may be an advantage to maintaining the fear. Is it motivating us to do something we do actually want or need, such as to look after our health or to take an exam? Is the fear we're experiencing temporary and clear in its intent? Only the right questions will reveal the truth, and we must see the truth of our fears to fully embrace them.

This is where great freedom dwells, individually and for collectives, enabling us to cultivate courage by going face-to-face with our fears, and feeling into what they can tell us. Only then can we replace our fear with the dreams that our true selves inspire and are waiting to bring forth.

Great leaps forward in our society have come from individuals who dismissed fear as the imposter it can be. Seeing your fears and challenging them with integrity takes a questioning mind, which can help you to question your subconscious, and to find great inspiration and freedom. Like a surgeon removing cancer from the body, the more incisive our questions, the more limitations and potential problems we remove.

You never know, the answers may surprise and delight you.

## The Normal Fearful Questions

Many of our leaders have unfortunately been conditioned to focus their attention on factors such as:

- Plans
- Outcomes
- Money/ financial profits
- Expectations
- Problems

Their questions are therefore derived from this level of normal awareness and focus. Is it any wonder, therefore, that the creative energies that can transform a collective are denied the attention they deserve, for they often come from a control perspective and are aimed at avoiding failure.

Let us consider some new types of questions that could replace these old favourites.

## Our Core Questions Reframed

### Our Need to Plan

Normally leaders will ask individuals in their collective to consider questions such as:

- Where and what will you/we be in one year, three years, and five years?
- Where are we at now, compared to our previous plans?

Stock standard questions like these take those involved out of the present and into the future. They tie us heavily to normal expectations.

Evolved leaders reframe these questions to take their collectives into a place of presence, in recognition that creation can only take place when we ourselves are fully present where we are. For example, an evolved leader might instead ask:

- What is the most valuable awareness, action, point of attention, or form of participation you/we can undertake right now to allow our creative possibilities to evolve?
- What is needed right now to inspire our team to be in its best place of creation?

These types of questions might take some answering, and challenge us to surrender to wonder, not worry. They represent a new paradigm, or way of opening.

When we come to accept that we really cannot predict the future with our minds, we can drop the fear of uncertainty that our obsession with time generates. We can both dream big, and bring our energy into the present, so that a platform of possibility is put in place. Dreams need doers to become reality, but first we must stimulate the dream so that it can be manifested. Dreaming is a feminine energy. Doing is masculine. We need both to birth possibilities into reality.

And perhaps life itself has a plan for us and, if we just listen in, we will hear it, rather than create a different one. After all, we are all just an aspect of the universe, and if we allow it to, it may take us to a whole new experience. This could quite literally be divine.

### Outcomes

Current leaders frequently ask:

- Are we achieving what we agreed to do?
- If not, who or what is to blame?
- Who or what needs to be punished or changed?

Evolved leaders consider these questions instead:

- How can we change HOW we are interacting and operating to enhance our ability to innovate, and exceed the goals we previously set?
- How can we help to lift the energy, and sense of fulfilment and well-being of our people so that their creativity, individually and as a team is significantly enhanced?
- What are our current energy levels like, and what might be stopping or stemming the flows of energy that create what we want?
- How can we inspire people right now to find their best creative ideas?
- How can we inspire greater harmonies to be present in our team, and from which we can create together?

These types of questions stem from taking accountability and understanding the power of being in the present moment. They are rich in inspiration and creativity.

A collective must consider the potency of its energy flows, before it even considers its outcomes. Positive flows of energy can create wonderful outcomes. Energy derived from inspiration is the creator, and we are it. We are the source of dreams.

Consider your car as an example. If your car is not running properly, you deal with the engine, because this is where the energy to stimulate motion comes from. You do not check out the headlights or the paintwork! We go to the source or heart of the problem to solve it.

In the same way, evolved leaders can choose to attend to the engine-room of the collective they are leading, and all that it interacts with, to get clarity on what can open their collective souls to stimulate the flow of creative energies. All in life is energy! Therefore, it is the flow of energy that creates and influences how one experiences life, people, and the collectives we interact with, and so on. It is all energetic, and intelligence flows from energy.

We have all heard the expression 'garbage-in, garbage-out' – thus the energy that flows into any collective will determine what flows out. Imagine what pure energy flowing from multiple creators could create! And pure energy is found in love and harmony, not in competition and fear.

When a leader's focus is on outcomes, and not the energy in motion within a collective, as expressed through e-motion, they severely limit possibilities and stifle innovation.

## Money

Wealth has a dominant place in many collectives due to our conditioning around money. Accordingly, any leaders wanting financial profit more than anything else will ask the following questions:

- How much money are we making?
- How do our results compare to our budgets and short- or long-term expectations?
- If we are not meeting budget, what do we need to do to make up the shortfall?
- How do we cut cost or make more money to meet our targets?

The focus is normally on the doing and outcomes. Counting the money is a critical activity in many large collectives – I should know, I was the Chief Financial Officer and auditor of multiple large corporate organisations! From my experience, great fragility arises when not enough money is being made, resulting in management feeling threatened, implementing accounting 'tricks', or charging customers more.

But are these pathways lacking in innovation and fresh thinking? As paths go, they are certainly well-trodden, but are they capable of leading us on new adventures? What if the focus was on enhancing the energy of the people involved, rather than sacrificing their well-being or creating a place of fear to turn things around.

Evolved leaders might try these questions instead:

- How can we inspire the people in our collective to create or help us to retain a greater abundance of money, without harming them?
- What energetic factors may be limiting the way any individuals involved perceive us right now, which might be restricting the flow for money?
- What can we learn as a collective from our experiences, so we can expand through the current circumstances as a unified collective and enhance our financial success?
- What truths do we need to express to lift our levels of creativity and hence our possibilities as a team?

When we only focus on what we can sacrifice to change an outcome, we lose the opportunity to ask what we can become to create greater possibilities. It's a powerful but subtle shift in approach.

Timelines might dictate how we approach any particular moment of dysfunction or disruption, but questions that go deeper into the way a collective feels and flows, can add much to its situation.

## Expectation, Expansion and Evolution

We are all inherently driven by the need to expand within ourselves; not just to acquire more things. However, our focus is often on the latter, because of the security it brings. This also applies to collectives on a grander scale. In fact, when lots of people come together within a collective, this focus can be amplified to new heights, challenging leaders in their application of the principle of expansion.

When I led people in business, I regularly sensed their fear of expansion, for expansion is a form of change, which most people prefer to avoid. Why? Because most minds prefer a comfort zone, rather than stepping into an unfamiliar place. This is not only normal, but it's what most individuals expect of their collectives – that it will remain familiar.

However, evolved leaders keep challenging this expectation, because they know that staying the same truly won't create the abundance that is possible for all. Great leaders therefore expect and encourage their collective to expand for the good of all, knowing that this includes their people, the planet, and others, potentially all around the world. How else will we evolve, if we don't keep imagining and creating?

In harmony we can all expand together, creating more for all, and this stems from the right energy, which in turn can find its foundation in better questions and shared listening. Positively charged energies, not limited by fear, can enhance the productivity and efficiency of a collective, in the same way that it does for an individual who loves their life and what they are involved with.

Positive energy in motion is an inspiration, particularly when based on a group of people loving what they are engaged in together.

The expansion of their followers is often not a priority for leaders, especially in business. Business leaders may often ask these kinds of questions:

- What is the minimum we have to do to meet our obligations in terms of team training and development?
- What types of expansion opportunities are needed to retain people and meet their expectations?
- Now that times are tougher, what can we delete from development activities to save money?

Whereas they, and all kinds of leaders, could be asking:

- What expansion or development will inspire our people, and lift the energies within our team?
- What learning will nourish the sense of purpose felt by our people, and make their lives feel more evolved and exciting?

- What expansion activities are in alignment with our desire to create a more inclusive culture, rich in well-being for our team?
- What expansion is needed to increase the self-awareness of our people, and our future leaders?

### Obstacles and Problems

It's quite easy in life to look for problems. Our current leaders are often masters at doing so, being well-versed in risk management and encouraged to find potential obstacles. But this mentality does not bode well for the human psyche, and our in-built desire for expansion. Looking for problems can be the father of fear, not the mother of invention.

We therefore need to change the rhetoric – away from obstacles and problems, to opportunities supporting growth and learning. This opens the gate to the well-lit pathway that lies ahead.

Current vernacular asks the following types of questions:

- What or who is going wrong, or is getting in the way of our preferred success levels?
- Who or what can we blame here (because it cannot be me)?
- Who needs to lose their current allocated position over this problem?

Current behaviours can sometimes be directed at blaming, and not necessarily looking for the energetic flows that could be enhanced by leaders striving to inject positivity, rather than fear, into a situation.

Blame serves no purpose, particularly if it leads to shame. We need to realise that we are never short of possibilities, we just think we are. Blame just introduces competition and fear into proceedings.

So what about asking questions like these instead:

- How should we communicate in the current circumstances

in order to inspire our team to embrace the learnings and opportunities that are currently upon us?
- How is the energetic alignment and motivation of our collective members contributing to our situation?
- What can we as leaders do to enhance the energy flows in the collective, so people feel more inspired, and create both collectively and more fully, despite our challenges?
- What will support wonderful emotions for the collective, instilling the power of creativity and joy in all, in these circumstances?
- Which team members may be struggling to find their full potency, and how can we help them to be more efficient and productive?
- What truths about ourselves are the current problems exposing for us to learn from?

If a leader can't go inward to search for truth, they are unlikely to manifest what is truly desired in the collective they lead. If you can't find your own truth, you are likely to struggle to embrace the truth of others.

In my own career, I built up a reputation for transforming low performing teams into high performing ones in record time, simply by changing the atmosphere within the teams. I hardly ever replaced the people, because to do so was based on a premise of blame. I simply strived to create harmony and higher levels of care in these teams, and to give people common purpose, trust and authentic levels of leadership. This was designed to allow them to evolve, in the best possible environment to support it. It worked every time, and it was not rocket science. People were never the problem. The environment they had to work within was the problem. Once the environment was improved, they were able to go to the levels of performance they truly wanted to be at, and then beyond.

Evolution is unstoppable in the long run.

## What Are We Doing to Each Other?

Collectives, whether they are businesses, families, societies or communities, can be harsh places to be if they are heavily controlled by fear.

We often harm each other through the overly competitive and uncaring way we treat each other. 'Dog eat dog', 'an eye for an eye', 'survival of the fittest' are all phrases that describe the highly competitive lives we have created for ourselves in many walks of life. There are many caring people in this world but, as a rule, we have morphed into a competitive and sometimes brutal culture. We all want more, more and more. It can be exhausting, especially when only the better competitors seem to excel. It often feels like it's 'every man for himself', and those sacrificed on the altar of supposed failure rarely forget, and may never forgive themselves. This can be a hard energy to let go. People are inherently loyal, but when they feel manipulated or let down, their loyalty is likely to be lost; at least to any leaders making them the 'scapegoat' for their collective's situation.

But instead of questioning who is to blame, or burying our heads in the sand to the plight of those struggling, we need to own our current situation. Let's be fascinated by our paradigms and get excited about the prospects we can ignite. Leaders are the key players who need to solve this dilemma, for they have the power to do so. They have the key to unlocking possibility, through channelling the combined energies of those they lead.

Fear is truly incapable of giving us the motives or emotions we need for maximum success. Care, love, and fun are the currencies we should be using to stimulate the flow of creative energy.

The universe is supportive of creative ideas that flow from love, and to the contrary, ultimately dismantles any creation that is out of alignment with truth.

In this environment, innovation is likely to be borne out of our inner senses as the word implies. It deserves our attention and applause.

So here are some big-picture questions we could ask for the good of all:

- What are we doing to ourselves, and to our own lives, with this often-cruel way of thinking and acting?
- What are we doing to each other?
- Why are we doing this?
- Are we wasting our lives being less happy than we are capable of being?
- Is that why we were born, to be less than what is possible?
- Can we individually and collectively put aside our historic propensity to accept suffering in our lives?

This type of thinking, when widely adopted, will require new leaders with new ways of thinking – authentic people who care about others more, not just themselves, and who can take responsibility for creating the right environments that all can thrive in. Such new and evolved leaders do step forward in our world, but we need more highly aware leaders, no matter how old they are. Wisdom can be found in a person of any age. Knowledge can come from experience, but knowing comes from the truth within us. It is embodied and felt.

This is about respect. It is about care. It's about compassion and about knowing that we are meant to enjoy life, not create a stressful experience for the masses just so the minority can have prestige, money, and the illusion of happiness. We are truly one big family sharing the journey of life together. Why treat each other with low levels of respect? We can be united as one, not just pretend to be!

We are all human beings living a life of purpose, and that purpose is to grow, expand, and live life as love. We are not here to be slaves to the rich and powerful, to give up our happiness in the blind hope that we will one day be one of the rich and successful people. In the end, only a small minority of people ever get to that lofty place many idolise. It is often said that 'it's lonely at the top' for a reason. Being the master of the destiny of others doesn't mean we have to switch off our natural sense of empathy and care.

A collective that truly gives its people the ability to be different and unique is one that understands the importance of authenticity. It allows its people to be who and what they really are. A collective that understands that people's lives matter immensely is one that is in touch with reality, and its people will be extremely loyal, and proud to belong to it. The strongest families come from this place. The strongest sports teams come from this place. The strongest businesses come from this place. This is our natural place.

During lockdowns, many people worked at home, rather than in the office. This has continued to some extent following the pandemic. Their productivity has been relatively high, with key tasks getting done, dispelling the previously commonly held belief that people could not be trusted to work at home, or out of sight. When collectives treat their workers like slaves, and without much loyalty, guess what they will get back?

The same goes for any collective. 'Rip customers off' and they will not forget easily what took place. Trust between consumers and selling organisations has become more strained. How often do you ring a supplier now, and the first thing you are told is that your call is being recorded for quality control purposes? Next time you hear this statement, why not tell them that you are also recording the conversation for your own purposes!

To create cultures that are more creative, requires leaders who can bring forth greater harmonies and truth that people can enjoy every day. This will unfold gracefully for us when leaders and their collectives ask the right questions, and listen with integrity to the answers that come forth.

Most people have their hearts in the right place. Give them the respect they deserve, and they will return it ten-fold.

It's time to be more incisive together, so we can cut through the densities many cultures are prone to possess. This will require the surgical removal of separation in our lives.

## 5.6 We Can't Handle the Truth

As a society, and as individuals, we often don't feel safe enough to identify and speak our truth. We all deeply crave the truth, but suspect it's a losing strategy, preferring to act rather than be our true selves. We may not even know what our fears really mean, because we haven't done the self-reflection to find out. Truth has become undervalued, and we have come to disrespect its power to set us free.

So why are we so afraid of the truth?

Brad Blanton, an American psychologist, explores and identifies the many widespread lies that dominate our lives in his book *Radical Honesty*, including all those little white lies that often deceive us. Indeed, we all lie to ourselves and the world sometimes, as a self-defence mechanism to protect or promote ourselves.

If we talk to others about our limitations or failures, for example, we may lose out, for the world may bear us limited compassion. In a competitive world, openly expressed honesty may be seen as a weakness, for it might makes us appear imperfect, which many of us fear. This is reasonable, because if life is a giant competition in which my survival depends on my ability to compete for limited resources, why would I risk my survival by always representing or telling the truth of my imperfections? Perfection will surely get me more.

For most people, the truth within them is thus a bridge too far to cross. It is a threat. So their minds convince them that a little white lie never hurt anyone. And as a result, society and its collectives have become a festival of lies and illusion at times, particularly in times of instability. There often becomes multiple versions of the truth, with truth being driven by opinions, which are in turn filtered through conditioned minds.

Many people lie for self-benefit. The media lies, our politicians lie, and why not if everybody else around me lies – why not lie too?

In the movie *A Few Good Men*, Jack Nicholson famously declares in a courtroom, "You can't handle the truth". He is right. We often can't handle the truth, because it risks us looking imperfect, it might shatter an image we seek to project, or challenge a comfort zone within which we have become entrenched.

But if we lie to ourselves on multiple fronts, imagine how challenging it is then to lead a collective with large numbers of people, all trying to preserve their reputations and acting out of alignment with their own real sense of truth? And imagine the complexity of this when you start to realise that most people do not even understand how and where they lie to themselves.

Jesus in the Bible (at John 8:32) reportedly said that "the truth will set you free". An exposed truth may cost us initially, but it is also energetically aligned with what and who we are, and ideally we need to live in alignment with our truth, which will always be known and felt in our hearts. It's our truth. No one else needs to agree with it.

Therefore evolved leaders need to ask what truths they might be scared of themselves and why, and how truth could set them free. For only once conscious leaders can truly focus on having integrity, can their people do the same. This is the road to real progress, and a highway to greater happiness. Substantial self-improvement is not possible in the absence of truth, for it blocks honest self-reflection, as an individual or collective.

If someone is fearful of being exposed by the truth, because of something they have done or not done, it is their responsibility to ask themselves:

- Why have I acted out of authenticity, and not done what was required?
- What inspired the behaviour that led to the less-than-ideal outcome or situation?

- What am I trying to protect or hide?
- What illusion am I identifying with and trying to create in the minds of others?

We need leaders with the courage and fortitude to call forth the truth in themselves and others. We need authentic leaders who can be true to who they are, no matter what circumstances arise.

Why does it require courage to be truthful in our society, when it's what we all want deep down, or at least say we want? Surely, we should need courage to lie, not to be truthful, because lying is energetically expensive, whether we realise it or not, and in a collective they are a form of pollution. It's a madness of our own making!

Our hearts know when we lie to ourselves or others. Lies stop us truly expanding to our fullness. They keep us trapped in mediocre relationships, for our intuition knows when we have been lied to.

The universe is never wrong. It never lies so why do we? It's time we stared this situation down, even if it requires us to be vulnerable. Our ability to expand to reach our maximum potential can only occur when we are authentic and true. The leaders we really need now are the ones who can stand in truth, honour it, and inspire those around them to do the same. Only these leaders can put an end to the illusions that hold us back from greatness – and a lack of truth in any situation is always linked to an illusion of some kind, creating diversions that lead us astray.

Relying on a lack of truth to create our world is ridiculous to say the least. Can you see the madness in this? Truth needs to be a flame we light in honour of ourselves, and what we are capable of being, always. A diversity of people will of course always have a diversity of truths, but we must respect those varying truths. This requires a culture full of open minds and hearts, where compassion for different perspectives is present.

To really transform our world to reach new and better paradigms, we must embrace truth. And there is no time like the present to be truthful. The true power of truth is a gift we can bestow upon ourselves.

Honestly, these distortions need to end. Our illusions have become delusions.

## 5.7 The Solidarity of Truth, Trust, and Purpose

Truth, trust, and purpose are deeply intertwined. In their unity, or solidarity, a leader and their collective can find the fluidity it deeply needs to be successful. All three attributes normally need to be found within the core of a leader, for them to become truly present and have maximum impact within a collective.

An advanced leader understands their true self, first and foremost. Self-awareness is the number one quality of any great leader. Self-awareness has no story and cares not about what, or who, we think we are; it simply contains our absolute truths, not what we have been taught about ourselves, or the world. It knows who and what we are, absolutely.

This is where we find our centre, and where we can open ourselves up to the truths of our lives. It overcomes the stories we seek to tell ourselves, which are often fantasies based on our ego. It is felt in our gut and sensed by our minds. It is the sun from which our lightness can shine forth.

Most of us have been taught to think our way through life, not to find reality inside our feelings, inside our bodies. We try to find it in our minds, which is not possible unless our beliefs already fully align with our truths.

But an advanced leader can sense into what is right. In the core of their intuition, they can find the truth within themselves, not outside themselves. They are the source of their own authority.

When a leader finds this truth – that they know they can trust – they can then bring this trust and truth to bear for the benefit of others.

It is in this core integration of truth and trust that the leader can begin to find their deeper calling, or purpose.

Trust is imperative in this. What would be the point of feeling your sense of truth if you couldn't trust in it? If you couldn't trust it, you would be unlikely to act on your desires or dreams.

Without knowing and trusting who they really are, a leader also risks being manipulated by their own mind. This would then cascade into the culture of their collective. When the mind takes over, it can bring false elevation to things like money, status, or importance.

Love can rewrite this script in our lives. If we love ourselves, we can live in alignment with our true intended stories, not the ones our minds or the minds of others conjure up.

### A Lack of Solidarity at Scale

When an individual leader cannot or will not access their core knowing, or trust it, the collective they lead will suffer.

But when a multitude of people within a collective are all detached from their core knowing, the issue is compounded on a grand scale. And this is where many collectives currently operate from, unfortunately.

If the leader cannot trust their own intuition, and does not know who or what they stand for, what chance do others have – to trust the collectives' direction and values, and know what they stand for. When there are a myriad of truths emanating from the egocentric minds of multitudes of people, who can they trust? And if they do not trust themselves or the consistency of message from others, a collective can become a swamp of distrust, where no one really knows what the collective stands for anymore. Truth, trust and purpose become disconnected and are not felt in unison by many.

It must all start with the leader going inward to find their own flow. Once this flow is found, it can cascade across the collective for the benefit of all, giving its members a rod of solidarity to follow and believe in. Once discovered, all can then flow together and share a common purpose. This is where collective happiness can be found, deep purpose can arise, and true productivity can take centre stage. They are intrinsically linked.

Exponential transformation – which has the power and intent to take us to new paradigms of success – has truth, trust, and purpose as key platforms at its centre.

Truth, trust, and purpose are also core ingredients of love. They are inseparable and can never be disconnected.

It's time we recognised the true power of truth!

## 5.8 A Chance to Self-Reflect

The concepts in this chapter are advanced in some ways, and to some readers may feel theoretical or abstract. However, we need to dream and step into our dreams with force to create new possibilities in this world.

Unless we open our minds to the creative ideas beyond our known experiences, how can we create more expansive opportunities? As Albert Einstein established, you can't solve a problem with the same level of consciousness that created it in the first place. So fresh thoughts can only arise from within more evolved beliefs and knowings.

So perhaps consider the following musings and questions:

- Do we really witness the purity of life being a priority in this world, and in fact in our history as a race? What do the plethora of wars and crimes suggest about the way we have historically led our lives? At the end of the day, we are causing this trauma!
- Up until the Covid-19 pandemic and the rise of the work-from-home concept did organisations sufficiently prioritise the home lives of their employees? Did you or your family suffer from the consequences of this?
- How often do we debate or consider what 'more' means in our

society, or our own lives? Do you really stop to consider what 'more' means to you and your family often enough?

- When you look around you, do you see spheres of equality or pyramids and rectangular structures that glue our minds to the illusion of status, and lead our lives to be like a serious game of snakes and ladders, where the consequences of landing on a 'snake' keep us trapped in a state of fear and competition rather than in a state of fun and collaboration?

- Does communication in our many collectives flow freely, or is it subjected to rules and flow in alignment with concepts of importance? In other words, he or she who matters gets to have a say; the rest get to listen and do what they are told. Can you relate to this?

- Do you ever feel hollow or fake, even after you have supposedly won what you have competed for? Do you or your collective only compete where you can be number one, or does being the best you can be and enjoying that experience matter just as much, if not more?

- Does the power of new 'left field' questions excite you, and could that help the meetings you take part in go to a whole new level of potentiality?

- Do you feel frustrated at times by the litany of image creation and distortions of truth you observe in life around you on a regular basis? Does it annoy you that the political leaders who shape your nation, and in turn your future, often sidestep the truth in search of votes and popularity?

- When you are forced to abandon or bend the truth, does it leave you feeling energetically harmed in some way?

- Can you imagine a world, or a collective, where truth is valued more than good news, always and for real?

- Can you draw a link between 'truth creating trust' in the collective environments within which you interact? How much trust do you really feel is embodied in the community where you live, or the workplace you attend? Would you like to see this change?

Again, your opinion matters, and I am merely playing the role of devil's advocate so together we can contemplate new possibilities. My role is to suggest these possibilities. Your role is to consider how you feel about them, and then form your own views.

Tangible transformation will only arise from the application of new levels of consciousness to current problems in this world. But first we need to break down the walls that stop us seeing where new horizons lie for us all. We need to climb the mountain to see what sits on the other side. Staying in base camp won't solve our current limitations and afford us new adventures, which we might all enjoy.

Read on and hopefully you'll see that what I think is aspirational in evolved collectives. But I ask you this: why should we settle for less?

# CHAPTER 6

## Stepping Stones to Harmony

This chapter sets out the key components of a great culture. These components represent the areas of key priority for the advanced leader to focus on, in order to create a wonderful ecosystem in which possibilities can be supported to become true realities.

Great leaders focus heavily and invest their energy into ensuring that their ecosystem is constantly rebalancing and being renewed, like nature does to a forest or its great oceans.

Collectives will never be perfect, and its components will always ebb and flow. However, consistent attention can ensure that it is as healthy as possible. The advanced leader knows that every ecosystem is based on the ongoing application of sensible and consistent decisions, not one-off or occasional forays into positive initiatives.

The key stepping stones, or qualities, that can create a cohesive collective are all interconnected, as this diagram suggests:

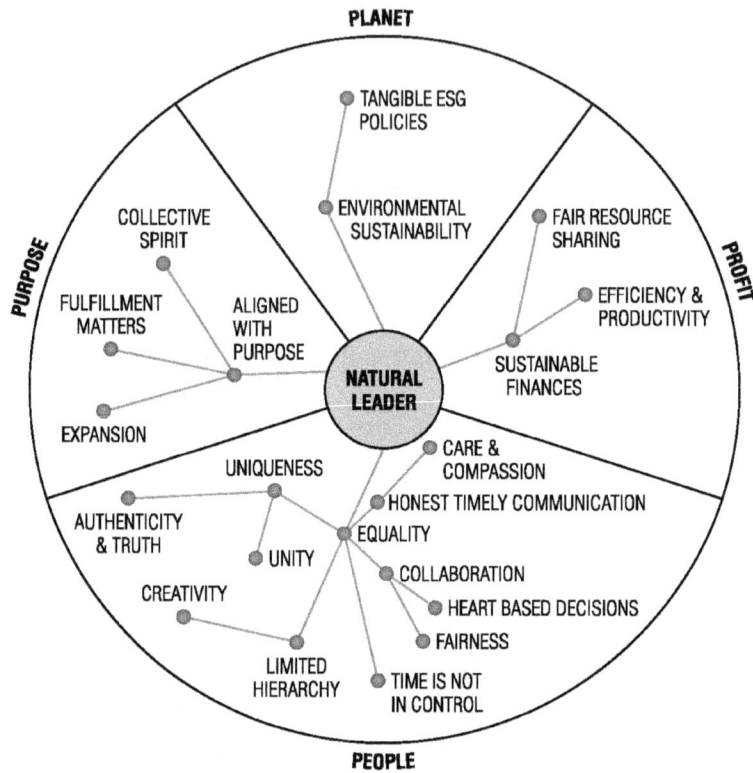

Figure 9: The Organism Generated by the Natural Leader

Balancing these components is a challenge for the conscious leader. But who doesn't like a challenge?

Let's consider them under the four Ps, being People – Purpose – Planet – and Profit.

## 1. People

Collectives often state that people are their greatest assets; but, despite this being true, some collectives do not align with what they espouse, particularly when times get tough.

People know when they are not being appreciated. You may have all the right words, systems, process controls and policies in place; but if those in a collective are not all appreciated equally, everyone will know it. We know when a collective's spoken intent is out of alignment with its actions and behaviours. Culture is king, as they say.

Let's consider some key areas that often require intention and attention. They are brief to avoid duplication with insights and ideas already expressed.

## Equality

This is a core quality that any collective must have to fully succeed. It is fundamental to unity and self-expression, for it allows everyone to be themselves, particularly those who might otherwise fear rejection in some way.

Judgement is the great separator within any collective, and when separation arises the potential for great teamwork becomes highly improbable. If a leader promotes, either through words or actions, that different people in a team are more important than others, competition and separation are inevitable, as individuals will strive to inflate their own positions within the collective.

A leader who cannot recognise that all in their collective are equally valuable, in their own way, and who believes that status and importance are more critical than the potency of the collective itself, is destined to deliver lesser outcomes than what are possible. Of course, some people in the collective may not make sufficient effort to be valuable, from a contribution perspective, and this must be addressed by the leader. But leaders who embrace equality whole-heartedly can build the kind of collective people will thrive within and love. If they do not, people will be forced to focus on competing within that collective, and in this place, you will often find unhealthy doses of fear and stagnation, as people avoid risk and consider other possibilities.

Without equality in a collective, fulfilment is unlikely for all.

## Collaboration

Our world is rife with competition, not collaboration. This causes much distortion within society.

I worked for a large organisation where collaboration was a genuine feature of the way the CEO and his key executives operated. The CEO did not tolerate unhealthy competition, and made collaboration a key performance indicator for all staff. The outcomes were dramatically positive for the organisation, and the result was positive outcomes for staff and customers alike. The CEO also reframed the concept for all staff, so that they saw themselves as being customers of each other. This was a master stroke and enhanced connection and unity.

## Uniqueness is Honoured

For human beings to be at their happiest, it helps if they can be truly authentic. This is possible with leadership that understands that powerful creativity can flow when people feel accepted and are not in fear of being themselves.

When a person needs to be something they are not, they are likely to be a shadow of what they can become, and in turn what they can contribute to a collective.

Leaders often recruit and support people in their own likenesses, and this can lead to a lack of diversity of thought and expression in a collective. 'Yes people' are great at preserving the status quo, but not so great at inspiring new paradigms of possibility, because a new type or level of awareness and thought is often needed to manifest transformation.

A lack of awareness of the power of uniqueness can be a huge inhibitor, and a great leader knows this and strives to eliminate it from the collective by role modelling acceptance.

## Honest Timely Communications

High quality communication is critical in all collectives.

When I worked in large corporate organisations, I often felt that much of the communications 'from the top' seemed to lack enough sincerity to touch those 'below', and to create real unity.

To really touch people, communications must be from the heart, and must address what the audience wants to hear or read about. It is not about leaders telling their people what they want them to know. It is about in-touch leaders knowing what their people need; and giving them honest information and feedback on what is required. You might call it a dose of reality, or a call to action.

Honest and useful communications are not patronising or insignificant. They do not skirt around the big or real issues that people want to know about. You cannot fool people, because the unofficial communication channels are always working overtime. People know when tough issues are being avoided.

Politics is a classic forum in which leaders communicate with spin and self-serving pronouncements. People know these communications are inauthentic, but after years of hearing it, many have given up listening. Politics needs a new breed of shepherds, who will communicate with honesty, integrity, and without spin. People are craving leaders with such power of presence, particularly if the media supports such authenticity.

## Care and Compassion

Many leaders in our society, particularly men, have been taught to lead with fear and powerful direction, all focussed on getting results. What many lack is the ability to really care about those they lead, because their focus is mostly on outcomes. This is a learned behaviour and can be unlearned.

As I've mentioned, I was a compassionate leader. I expected good outcomes, but I always led with great care. I cared about the lives of my people, including their health, their home lives, and so on, and they sensed that. And in return they cared about me. Respect and care flowed in both directions.

Every action has an equal and opposite reaction. So when you do not genuinely care as a leader, guess what you will get in return? Sure, things will get done, because most people will do what must be done, because they are committed to their tasks. But when they feel abused or exploited, they will most likely lose respect for their leaders. They may not express it openly, but it will erode their loyalty.

Returning to our shepherd analogy, the evolved shepherd cares about the flock as much as their own self. They meet perceived failures with compassion, for they know when the flock is being courageous. Their own courage is also met by their own self-compassion and care. The flow of care and compassion must be spherical, travelling in all directions in a collective for harmony to be felt.

The shepherd does not allow the flock to walk off a cliff, face the wolves alone or atrophy in a field where food has become scarce. They care for their flock without worrying that might be perceived as soft and fluffy.

Care is also not just about those within a collective. It must be externally focussed too, on competitors, regulators, suppliers, customers, and so on. This care can be in short supply.

### Limited Hierarchy

Most collectives need a management hierarchy for practical reasons. However, this need is over-played, and reflects our human need to be seen to have a certain level of importance or elevation. Great leaders know there must be a hierarchy of some kind. Not everyone can attend a board meeting! Not everyone in a family can have responsibility for decisions. However, such leaders also abandon the hierarchy concept when interacting with those in their collective, so they can be present with everyone, and live true to the equality that's needed for success.

Being a leader does not make you better than a follower. You are more likely to be older, or more experienced.

When I first reached a reasonably senior rank, my staff found it curious that I would make tea and coffee at times for junior staff. I just did it naturally, because I come from a place of equality, but many had not seen this before from an executive. The subliminal message was powerful. The act was minuscule.

## Unity

For human society to flourish it needs unity. Within any collective, unified people will always achieve more than individuals in isolation.

In most collectives, real unity is difficult to achieve because of the inherent propensity for many involved, including some leaders, to be motivated by self-interest. 'What's in this for me' might best describe a common mentality. This one is a hard one to smash, because of the subconscious propensity for people to seek outcomes outside themselves, before they can feel good about themselves. Everyone will say they are a team player, but some people still struggle to be, particularly in times of pressure, and need to be induced to act in the collective's best interest, particularly if it conflicts with their own needs.

Inspiring leaders get everyone in their collective to see that working together, and supporting each other, is in the best interests of all involved, regardless of title or level! The leader enunciates clearly and practically what is to be gained from taking a united team approach and acting with a united front. Once people feel that this unity is real, it can create a positive experience for them. It is a natural place that people crave to be in.

I once took over the leadership of a team where few people knew each other. Their reputation and outcomes as a collective were less than ideal to say the least. My first task was to give everyone the opportunity to get to know each other, and to trust each other. And I had to model this, by being similarly committed to the unity I encouraged. Being vulnerable in all that I did then allowed others to be vulnerable, and created trust across the team. If the boss attends functions and is truly present, it encourages others to do the same, and to take off the masks they may have previously felt the need to wear. I even went as far as to sing in front of my staff for fun. Now, I can't sing, but it did build trust, for I was being vulnerable and my imperfections as a singer were clearly on display.

Great sporting teams often win because they have mastered unity as a practice. They are 'tuned' into each other and don't compete with each other for the limelight.

## Heart-Based Decisions

For any collective or leader to achieve their full potential, they need to make decisions that emanate from their hearts, not just their minds.

People know when a leader's decision is built on self-interest, when it is not based on compassion or care, or when it does not value human rights. People may not complain or express the pain of such unfair decisions, but they know when they have been directed inappropriately.

Heart-based decision may result in something less profitable being achieved, but they are most likely to align with your values or governing principles, and therefore will be more sustainable in the long term.

Early in my career as a leader, I struggled at times to make decisions, for I did not fully trust my intuition. This led me to a place of excess analysis and opinion seeking, before I would see a course of action. As I progressed in experience, I learned to trust my gut feel much more. This allowed me to make decisions with more conviction, timeliness, and surety.

When you make consistent and sensible decisions over time, you end up with a sensible collective, and are more likely to get the outcomes desired, because you have sensed into your wisdom to find the right decision for the situation at hand, and test-checked it with a logical mind. The heart and mind need to work together for wholeness to be achieved. They need each other to generate success.

## Creativity is Honoured

The best leaders know that fresh ideas are magic for any collective, even if they come from the most junior team members. They know that continuous and exponential improvement requires new ideas and an ongoing commitment to expansion.

Often the more 'junior' members of a collective are the creative ones, and they need to be honoured with their involvement in creative activities.

In large collectives, it may be the person who writes computer code, or works in a customer-facing role, who knows what will really be effective and create new possibilities. But alas, they may never be consulted for their view, despite it being valuable, because of their perceived lack of seniority.

If a leader thinks that only their senior people can create innovative ideas and continuous improvement, they will shut down enormous potential.

When I was in senior roles, I would always strive to invite my team members to have input into strategy sessions at initial stages. I ensured creativity was rewarded, regardless of its scale. This is only possible of course if collectives are not too big to make this impractical.

My most recent team also conducted monthly idea sessions with all team members, which we called the 'Hour of Power'. It helped to generate new ideas, and create new initiatives on key matters. This allowed everyone to feel engaged in the development of our business offerings, further contributing to unity. We used to pick one idea each month to try and implement it, assuming it was practical to do so.

## Control Time, Don't Let It Control You!

It's easy as a leader to set deadlines that you ideally think are preferable, and most likely will assist your image. However, a great leader constantly feels into the energy of the collective that they are leading, and knows when deadlines need to be reset.

People matter, not just outcomes. Sometimes deadlines cannot be moved, because they are set by more influential forces or bodies, even lawmakers. However, knowing when to reduce demands on people is critical to maintaining morale. It's the people who ultimately create the money and success.

The well-being of people is paramount, and even if you cannot honour it in the thick of the action, you can always do so after the event to compensate for the sacrifice people make, beyond what is reasonable.

As a leader I always set ambitious plans for my team to provoke improvement, and challenge. However, I felt into the mood of my team every day to sense when deadlines needed to be moved, when more resources needed to be gained, or when people needed to be given rewards or time off to regather their energy for the next challenge. This helped them to feel honoured.

Some people say 'time is money', but this statement belies the fact that people are your greatest conduit to success, and they cannot be allowed to feel undervalued or manipulated relative to money. Unfortunately, this is all too common in a lot of collectives.

## Fairness

Fairness is critical in any collective, and once the treatment of people across the collective is perceived as favouring some over others, cultural deterioration will take place. Fairness is a close cousin of equality.

The 'boys club' is often quoted as being an issue in collectives historically, including government. This can occur when men favour other men, who behave or enjoy similar interests. I have witnessed it myself a number of times.

The full commitment of everyone in a collective is more likely if it is stimulated by fair treatment – be it salary, feedback, rewards, or the leader's time.

## 2. Purpose

### Alignment with Deep Purpose

A purpose is a core belief or thought. Why do we exist? What do we do for people or ourselves? What gives us fulfilment? How do we truly succeed (other than through making money)? Purpose needs constant reinforcement and reflection in a collective to drive sustainable outcomes, or it becomes just a nebulous thought. Purpose may be complex or simple. In an individual's case, it may be as simple as being happy or being loved.

Most businesses have a purpose, which translates into the products or services they provide or sell. It may be to provide care or support, banking services, or insurance products to protect people, for example.

Most families have a purpose, which translates into ensuring the health, well-being and prosperity of a unified and authentically happy group.

Most sporting groups form with a purpose – whether it's to win every game, or to enjoy active fun together as a collective.

Whatever a collective's purpose is, it needs to be understood and embraced by everyone in order for that collective to be successful to the fullest extent possible. Most collectives start out with a clear purpose in mind, which may expand along with their suite of activities. But over time, the true purpose of a collective can often get diminished and overshadowed by a desire to make money or to win over competitors. This is not surprising in a world driven by competition, where money is a source of validation for so many people, and thus the collectives in which they live and work.

But when a collective steps out of alignment with its values and core beliefs, it steps out of integrity, and most of those involved see it and feel it. The subconscious beliefs of each individual play a part in this, influencing their actions and behaviours.

For this reason, a priceless exercise is to look closely at organisational beliefs, rather than just setting rules and requirements, and see how those are being expressed through the collective's actions and behaviours. Do they actually align with the collective's purpose for existing? Has that purpose changed over time? Is everyone aware of that purpose? Does everyone actually believe in it?

An evolved leader will regularly review their collective's purpose and ensure it aligns with everyone's values. Purpose should not just be a hope put into words and hung on a wall. It needs to be deeply felt and owned.

### Cultivating a Collective's Spirit

The human spirit guides our lives. Whether knowingly or unknowingly, it is an enduring motivator that can be accessed through our hearts. We often talk about it, though it is an abstract concept not truly admitted to by our minds. Often our spirit is brought forth in moments of disruption or change. It brings our inherent strength to the fore.

A collective is the aggregation of the spirits of those involved with it. In this way, the spirit of a collective is magnified, when compared to the spirit of an individual, making the task of a leader even more profoundly important, but challenging.

If leaders do not consider the core spirit of a collective, random outcomes are more likely to eventuate, and these random outcomes will reflect the random beliefs of the people within the collectives. Thus evolved leaders spend time and energy creating an alignment of spirit within their collective. We sometimes refer to people as spiritual or not. But this belies the fact that we are all spirits living a physical life.

The only difference between a so-called spiritual and non-spiritual person is their level of awareness about what they truly are.

Accordingly, great leaders devote much of their energy to inspiring their people.

### The Potency of Expansion

The opportunity to expand, not just inflate for external recognition or reward, needs to be at the heart of every collective to make it meaningful for those involved. This type of expansion comes from truth and our inherent nature.

Deep in our hearts we all seek to evolve. This involves learning more about the truth of who and what we really are, what we are capable of becoming, and learning from experiences (rather than seeing them as problems or failures). At its very core, it's a return to a more loving way of living, because at our core we are all pure love. Our hearts know this, if we allow them to show us!

Inspiring leaders know the power of expanding the collective, and those involved in it, through every experience. When expansion, or growth, is the key desire in everything that a collective does, sustainable and conscious improvement can take place for the benefit of all. To do this properly means opening up to the feelings in a collective, not just their thoughts, and encouraging the collective to embrace the energy of gratitude when things go wrong. Humans tend to learn better from hardship than success, unfortunately – although of course it's possible to learn from both. And all that we experience is truly a gift to learn from. Therefore, any mishap (unless it is terminal) is a chance for expansion.

Very aware collectives, led by advanced leaders, can embrace this through integrity with enthusiasm, arising from the joy of learning and continuously improving.

Fundamentally we all want to be more, not just own more.

## Fulfilment Matters

Commensurate with the need for purpose, many collectives seek to define their success by reference to metrics outside themselves.

Have we lost our desire for fulfilment and fun in life and business? Do we really think seriousness creates wealth? Can't we have fun and still be successful? Does productivity have to come from sacrifice and perspiration, or can it come from pleasure and inspiration?

The search for productivity has been defined as getting more out of the same resources, or even less resources. Yet so often we work long hours and sacrifice our personal time and sense of ease to get things done. We do this because we are afraid for our security, whereas a far more potent motivator is fulfilment. It arises when our hearts are full of love for what we are involved in, and when a leader can inspire and excite people to contribute.

Evolved leaders understand the unlimited possibilities of freedom and joy.

# 3. Planet

## Environmental Sustainability

The conscious leader knows that our planet matters and should not be deprecated upon in the quest for advancement. Balance is the key, as it is in all aspects of life.

For many years, a lot of larger collectives have half-heartedly purported to care for the planet; but now many investors and interested stakeholders, including members of the public, are taking this to a whole new level and demanding action by every large collective, including governments. The younger generations in particular seem to be more in touch with ecological considerations; the older generations having grown up at a time when global warming was seen as the domain of alarmists and green zealots. But, no matter what activity a collective is involved in, every collective has a responsibility to care for the planet.

The conscious leader understands this, and knows that all decisions need to explicitly take account of environmental factors and risks. This needs to have real substance to it, and not just appear to be taking account of environmental factors. This can require great courage and integrity, for it may impact on short-term financial profits, but it is necessary. There is no point in valuing people, having purpose, or being rich if your health or livelihood is threatened by ecological deterioration. Money is not very valuable if we are dying off, unless you own a funeral business!

### Tangible ESG Policies

Over the last few decades, many business organisations have been forced to comply with rules relating to Environmental and Sustainability Guidelines (ESG). Regulatory requirements often dictate what is required in this regard.

The move to ESG policies and practices is a good thing, for it has given organisations and investors a way to move forward, and a lens through which to assess organisational alignment with climate change imperatives.

However, this remains a developing and important field of organisational development. ESG is clearly a positive step in the right direction. However, it is incumbent on great leaders and organisations to approach ESG with the right intent, to do the right thing for the planet, not to just meet minimum standards for the sake of disclosure and as a way of self-promotion.

Substance over form is critical in this space.

## 4. Profit

In balancing the 4 Ps, this P has great prominence, so much that it has become a principal 'P' for many. This is very understandable, given what money can do for our lives.

But money is easier to take or fake, than to make, and many spend their lives pursuing it without much conscience. People steal for it, kill for it, or act without integrity to attain it. People sacrifice their health and time with their loved ones to pursue it. Of course these people are conditioned and need understanding, not criticism. We must have compassion for their plight, for the source of this mentality is likely to have been imposed upon them. What they fail to understand is that there will never be 'enough' money, so the more crucial question is: how do we narrow the gap between rich and poor, without taking away the incentive for people to create wealth?

Wealth should not be a proxy for the value of any person or a collective of people.

Unfortunately, conditioned thinking has distorted this principle. Greed, not the concept of sharing, has taken centre stage in many regards.

Money is not the problem in itself. It is a wonderful energy in our lives. It is a great way to value work, but not people.

## Sustainability of Finances

Renewal is critical for sustainability and survival. Yet many collectives fail to see the value in renewal.

As the recent Covid-19 pandemic showed us, many larger collectives could not sustain such a major downturn or disruption. Short-term thinking had led to many collectives making short-term decisions to maximise financial profits, without considering the challenges that could lay ahead. Fortunately for many, governments saved them in the pandemic with hand-outs.

As we each consume in search of instant gratification, are we the same? Do we put enough resources aside for a 'rainy' day? Do we spend enough time looking into the future, to search for the next field that will sustain our herd? No one field can feed a flock forever. We must be like the shepherd always looking for new, clean, and fertile fields of sustenance, to keep our collective alive and safe. We must evolve to thrive. Wisdom can arise in stillness and joy, but not wealth – we must step into newfound wisdom to create wealth.

This requires high quality risk management, an eye to alternative opportunities through quality strategies, and an open mind to fresh ways of thinking. It requires ongoing investment in the future, not just an obsession with having more now. It requires capital levels being sufficient to support future viability. It is always a balance, and it's a task within which the balanced leader finds inspiration. Their flock needs them to direct energy here. It's not enough to just philosophise, we must activate the possibilities.

### Fair Sharing of Resources

The haves and the have-not's principle is always likely to apply; however, our society could be much fairer in the way resources are shared.

There is great scope for the haves to direct more resources into helping the have-nots. The herd that shares its sustenance most likely survives the winter together!

There is a point where the current paradigm of have and have-nots breaks down. The haves only have because, to some extent, the have-nots support them. When you push the have-nots to a breaking point, in large enough numbers, the haves will surely suffer too. This tends to occur in significant economic downturns, like a recession or depression, because markets for equities, currencies and other assets become volatile and fall. And unemployment rises.

The bottom line is that we need each other for prosperity, and when we forget we are truly one, and create too much separation and division, the current financial systems can 'snap', harming both the rich and the poor. Of course, the poor will suffer more as they have less to fall back on in difficult times.

Successful collectives that fail to treat their people fairly, soon get themselves offside with those they serve. For example, when workers within a collective are underpaid for too long – like teachers, miners or nurses – or their value is not recognised – like creatives – they will give up, or lower the passion they have for their position. No one ultimately wins in this circumstance.

There is considerable evidence that, over recent decades, corporate profits and productivity levels have been increasing at a faster rate than salaries for workers. This is causing distress for the average person, particularly when it coincides with cost increases for essential goods and services like energy, food, housing, medical services, education and so on. New technologies have also seen creatives under-paid for their work, such as writing for streaming services; or not paid at all. This is neither fair, nor sustainable. If we wish to consume their services, they must be paid properly for their work.

According to the Economic Policy Institute (EPI), in a report issued in 2021, productivity in the USA grew between 1979 and 2020 by 61.8%, whereas the hourly pay of workers rose by 17.5% (after adjusting both for inflation). That is a 350% difference, or 3.5 times, and translates into higher corporate profits.

The story in Australia is the same. A report by Acuity in 2018 showed that between 2000 and 2018 productivity in Australia rose by 26%, while real wages only rose by 13%.

In New Zealand over the same period, productivity rose by 23% and real wages remained unchanged (after adjusting for inflation).

The sharing of rewards is clearly unfair in all three economies and needs to be addressed.

So why has this gap eventuated and made life so much harder for many workers?

The EPI report in America attributes this to a loss of worker power in salary bargaining. The report states that:

> "In the 1970s, policymakers began dismantling all the policy bulwarks helping to ensure that typical workers' wages grew with productivity.

Excess unemployment was tolerated to keep any change of inflation in check. Raises in minimum wages became smaller and rarer.

After 1979 productivity grew at a significantly slower pace relative to previous decades. But because pay growth for typical workers decelerated even more markedly, a large wedge between productivity and pay emerged."

The report concluded that economic growth slowed over the 40+ years analysed, but was also allocated on a radically unequal basis.

It further concludes that the extra financial profits have largely been allocated to:

- Salaries of the top 20% of workers (ie. executives)
- Shareholders in the form of rising share prices and dividend income

There is only one fix for this problem. Businesses need to allocate a higher share of productivity gains to workers, not just to executives and shareholders.

This is only likely to occur through more compassionate leadership. I'm not saying leaders won't be paid more than less senior workers, just that the allocation of financial profits needs to be fairer.

If this is not done, we run the risk of both workers and businesses suffering in the medium to long-term. If businesses do not allocate a fairer share of the financial profit pie to workers in the future, they will suffer too, because people will not be able to afford their products, and because people will withdraw their labour all together through strikes, or more long-term career decisions.

In my career as an executive, I was witness to several payroll reviews and processes to reset staff salaries. Typically staff were given an annual increase in salary of say 2% to 3%, regardless of the growth in financial profits. Executives' pay rises were somewhat similar, but many had bonus potentials that could substantially increase their normal salaries. Bonuses of staff further down the pyramid were a fraction of this.

Business collectives can only afford so much in salaries, but the differentials between leaders and workers have become extreme in some cases. No wonder everyone wants to be in the leadership ranks!

Businesses may reprice to offset rising costs or higher salaries, but this just means the more vulnerable members of society are at their mercy and will struggle to get ahead collectively. The merry-go-round then continues and never ends, resulting in few real winners, except those larger collectives with significant repricing power.

Highly evolved leaders of the future must understand that abundance must be shared more fairly than it is now. To do otherwise is to disrupt the flow of positivity within a collective of people, and dismiss the power of unity to create even greater abundance.

### Efficiency and Productivity

To achieve both efficiency and productivity, collectives must make changes for the good of all.

Productivity for many current business collectives is often interpreted as getting staff to do more with less, and that less is often applied in the form of less people, creating cohorts of overworked people, and making others 'redundant', causing great emotional distress all round.

In the 1990s, Jack Welsh made a name for himself by increasing the financial success of the US company General Electric. He would get rid of the least effective 10 percent of the workforce each year, regardless of their contribution. I worked for a CEO who tried to apply this principle. It caused intense stress for staff, and was uninspiring for most people involved, for it stimulated unhealthy competition and the fear of career annihilation.

I found myself working long hours, travelling, and being under intense pressure at times. It impacted on my health, my marriages, my relationship with my children, and my self-esteem. However, I rarely admitted this to anyone. I just kept going, putting my employers first in my life. Yes, I got success in terms of money and title, but in hindsight it wasn't worth it. I don't blame my employers. I chose this, out of a fear of failure.

From a business perspective, this process also failed to create real efficiency or productivity. Efficiency comes, not just from lower costs, but from people in a collective interacting with each other at the right time, in the right way. This should result in inspiration and greater enjoyment for staff, not just in more money for a collective. Productivity is then always higher when those involved are motivated through a sense of fulfilment, when they love what they're doing. Productivity motivated by fear is unreliable and unsustainable, and thus cannot generate true expansion. Money without substance and devoid of productivity gains can only ever be inflationary, not expansive in the long run.

The advanced leader knows that financial profits are more likely to be repeated and grow when real productivity and efficiency are built into systems and processes, not left to arise from the unnatural sacrifices of those programmed to operate from a place of fear. A collective operating with inspiration and true purpose will create greater wealth for all on a macro level. True leadership based on new levels of equality and wisdom will ensure this.

This is an exciting prospect and can align our society with a new cocktail of possibilities. Everything in life has the power of possibility embedded within it. Future generations of leaders can come from a place of knowing that nothing is perfect, but that everything can continue to evolve.

The highly self-aware leader must thus be fully aware and care about the whole ecosystem; not just the privileged few who have traditionally held power at the top of the pyramid. To do otherwise is ultimately unsustainable.

# CHAPTER 7

## Our Opportunity to Transform Together

If you have read this far, you are most likely motivated to consider what more leadership can create when based consciously on love and truth. You may have already begun your own personal transformation journey, or perhaps you are in a collective that is receptive to changing traditional paradigms of leadership. Perhaps both apply.

The contents of this book may resonate with you, and you may be motivated to apply some of its principles to relieve the pain and discomfort you or others might be experiencing as a result of traditional leadership practices and beliefs.

Perhaps you are a senior leader, or someone aspiring to be, and you want to make a difference in this world.

Perhaps you are a community leader helping people to move after significant disruption or hardship.

Perhaps you are a family leader who seeks to be more supportive of the collective, so you can thrive together for years to come.

Whatever the reason, I applaud your curiosity.

What I have attempted to do in this book, is to paint a picture of different ways of leading, living, and transforming. All is possible when we broaden and expand our awareness levels. It is the key to the advancement of humanity, to experience and unlock new ways of being and create new versions of more.

There are no right or wrong answers to guide our futures, just stepping stones on the journey of continuous improvement, which are ever unfolding as our self-awareness expands alongside it.

Our search for 'more' has traditionally been focussed on increasing the quantity or quality of outputs from collectives, so we can own more. But the game of life we have played can always be transformed as we transform ourselves, and go to reach new levels of awareness. We can be more, enjoy more, and love more – not just have more. It is time we redefined the meaning of more?

This book is not intended to criticise the past, although it offers critiques to provide a suitable point of reference from which possibility can arise. And I do not hide from the fact that I was very much a part of the past I am critiquing. It took me many years to consider all this and transform myself, and my long-held beliefs.

Relaxing into a new and different future is the key. Awareness is easier to access from a state of relaxation, as it opens the door for truth to be found within us all. It requires genuine self-reflection. We have to let go of the need for any predetermined outcomes, for the reality is that opportunities will only present themselves to us when we reach a suitable level of awareness to perceive and receive them. This takes patience and an open mind to allow our hearts to show us what is possible. We must open to new ways of thinking and expressing what we feel!

Traditional ways of discovering our next steps will provide us with limited opportunities, for those usually involve thinking and planning, most likely under the pressure of deadlines. This has been our normal way of operating. So we must instead allow space to be present in our ways of operating, to open the door to fresh ideas. Creating space to disengage our minds temporarily allows us to be truly present in our lives and to create. Our minds are great implementers, and this is the key role. It's hard to bring new things into a place of stress and clutter. Space allows for relaxation and exploration, for in this void our imaginations can take over and do what they do best.

Patience is truly a strength, not a weakness; although taking suitable periods of time to be actively open to fresh ideas has not been a normal paradigm familiar to most of us. We have been taught instead that 'time is money', and that we must get things done as quickly as possible – these are the badges of honour we all wear. I know I did for much of my life.

But what if concepts and offerings can be better served by working alongside our ever-expanding conscious awareness, to allow it to take us to new heights? And what if we truly can't see what is going to arise until it enters our peripheral vision?

To properly apply this new paradigm of creation to our collectives, we desire harmony and unification as key ingredients capable of supporting real expansion. None of us can be heroes and do it alone! None of us have all the answers or best ideas to enhance our world, so a collective of people coming together to explore better ways to improve is always going to provide a better chance of finding great ideas to manifest into reality.

Separation and competition between people within a collective is not likely to maximise the quality or quantity of fresh ideas. When we have unhealthy levels of competition within a collective, we ultimately become our own opponents. We get in the way of ourselves. It's hard enough to stand out in any walk of life and improve your offerings, without trying to do so with self-imposed barriers and limits.

Collaboration is an essential ingredient of collective success, but it is borne out of meaningful connection between human beings that creates trust, for it changes the chemistry of interactions. It infuses love, not fear, into a situation, and can take us on a more enjoyable journey of discovery. In a world where judgement of each other can be excessive at times, we often find ourselves being forced into a place of protection and projection.

To maintain our reputations, we often feel the pressure to protect ourselves from blame, and to put forward an image we think will serve us in competitive situations. Image management is rife in our world because we have all had to do it to some extent to survive. But imagine a world in which we can each be our true selves, not a conjured-up version of ourselves to satisfy the expectations of others.

## Your Sphere of Influence

The sphere has a wonderful capability to expand and flow as it rolls forth, through a series of present moments to create our future.

As a leader in the present moment, you have the opportunity to influence how you and your collective flows and grows. Your sphere of influence is one that will probably grow as your awareness expands.

I have introduced into this book a series of core ingredients that I believe could take you to new paradigms if embraced. However, by definition they are advanced and may threaten some. From my experience, such unfamiliar ideas can often create an initial period of ambiguity and doubt. Being and believing differently can feel strange, and somewhat isolating. You don't conform with the herd anymore, and it can feel like you are swimming against the tide. You are different – but not wrong. This has certainly been my personal experience. There is no right or wrong; all is a choice.

We can't know exactly where we will end up, for that is not what our hearts truly want. They want an adventure with no self-imposed limits, and one in which all who choose to engage can revel and feel joyous and relaxed in the experience. Here, they can be present and offer creative ideas that complement our growing awareness levels.

Leaders within a collective are also individuals who have a life to lead. If they have integrity in the way they lead their own lives, they will be in alignment with how they lead others. Any other way of being will be seen as lacking authenticity by those who follow.

## Recapping the Key Ingredients

There are a number of concepts introduced through this book to enhance the possibility of collective happiness, and therefore the happiness of individuals.

Each collective is comprised of the sum of unique individuals. The sum of the microcosms must add to the totality of the macrocosms we share.

The following core ingredients are the cornerstone of the 'more' we are capable of creating. Where these ingredients may be lacking in the recipe of life, they can however add up to a less-than-ideal menu of experiences from which we can choose.

Isn't it time to spice them up, so we can experience new and exciting versions of 'more'?

These ingredients include greater infusions of:

- Unity, not separation
- An appreciation of the true power of truth
- True connection that far exceeds basic levels of contact
- Truth and integrity, to allow greater trust to descend
- Respect for the value and purity of human life
- Equality through greater inclusion and sharing
- Collaboration, not competition, that recognises the creative talents of all
- Respect for the importance of well-being
- Care and empathy
- Patience, not clock watching
- Forgiveness, not the blame game
- Acceptance, not judgement
- An openness to more expansive questions
- A focus on balancing: purpose, people, profit, and the well-being of the planet
- Sustainability, not necessarily maximum performance at all times

- A broader definition of what constitutes success
- Expansion and learning as a core part of how we operate, rather than results and inflation being the primary focus
- Decision making that is intuitive before it is logical, but ultimately relies on both
- The acceptance of feelings and emotions as a source of truth in any collective, which requires more feminine energies to arise
- A willingness to love and embrace fear, and hear what it has to tell us, rather than suppress it; for fear is merely a wonderful indicator we can harness – it is full of wisdom
- Leaders who seek to preside over important work, not be important themselves
- A need to treat everyone as you seek to be treated yourself
- A desire to reject suffering in our lives, rather than cling to it as a badge of honour
- A greater focus on wisdom and health, not just wealth
- A deeper contemplation of the 'more' we are really seeking
- Love for all of the above stems from within its unlimited power to create

Current leadership tends to deprioritise many of these as they instead focus on results, not the experience being created. This is because of the pressure we are all under to win and deliver outcomes. We are in a cage of conditioning of our own making, yet we hold the keys that can set us free. Leaders with higher levels of personal consciousness must be the key drivers of this transformation in society. This requires an understanding of the power of transformation over our propensity to fear change and new paradigms.

A leader who is prepared to invest time and energy in their own transformation first, can then bring forth all they become into a collective of people and lead the way.

I have no doubt that, as a leader transforms, they can and will create a new version of themselves that will allow authenticity to take centre stage and forge a new level of harmony in any collective they lead. Any accomplished leader needs to be clear on what kind of life they and their people wish to lead. This can arise from deep self-reflection, and the 'self' I am referring to here is found in our hearts, or intuition. It is our source of truth.

With every lift in harmony, comes a greater chance that possibilities will be imagined, and can be brought into reality in any collective, like a fine concert. We are all creators in our own right, and a leader that recognises this and brings all to the table equally, to contribute to the creation process, can become the centre of creations in their own team of creators.

As an individual and leader who has walked this path myself, I stand ready to assist any leader who wants to know more, and be more for the good of all. Please visit my website for more details.

We are all the creators of our own experience, and we can only ever be what our level of awareness allows. Higher self-awareness creates the dawning of possibility and, like the sunrise, it is possible with every new day. It has the potential for constant rebirth and resurrection. As we expand our awareness, we can create a better future for all.

I hope all leaders reading this find that concept incredibly motivating. I know I do.

We can all perform adequately when times are good, but it is a whole new adventure for a leader to embrace transformation made necessary by dysfunction. Staring disappointment and 'failure' in the face, and approaching it with powerful resilience and a fresh perspective borne out of higher levels of self-awareness, is an incredibly satisfying place for a leader, and for the collective they lead.

This book invites you into a more welcoming place of power and peace. And this power comes from the power of love. You owe this to yourself, so you can then offer it to others!

# CHAPTER 8

# Concluding Remarks

## 8.1 Can the Wise Leaders Please Step Forward

My career in the business world and my observations of society have shown me much. I will always cherish the opportunities I was given in my career and the wonderful benefits it provided me with, so that I could support my family and myself.

But with all the positives I received, and the great people I met, my involvement in the business world and in my personal life was often emotionally challenging. I own these experiences, for I chose them.

Fear was a common ingredient I encountered in the business world. However, I did not perceive this fear for much of my career. It wasn't until later on in my life that I was able to see it for what it was. Behind my stoic face, calm exterior and smiles was a litany of emotions, including stress. I did my best to be authentically me, but it took a long time to work out who or what that meant, and to have the courage to step into this truth.

I can forgive myself for what I was, as I was the product of my upbringing, and the expectations of the society in which I grew up. But I have since reprioritised what I valued, and focussed on what interested me, and I'm now a much happier person.

I did have great success in transforming the teams I led, because I believed with great passion in unity, truth, equality and the value of people's lives, and I made sure I led with these principles in my heart and mind. I needed always to transform myself first and foremost, before I could apply what I learned to my role as a leader, partner, or father.

My commitment to transformation has never been deeper than it is today, for my desire to evolve is at the forefront of my life. I know in my heart that this is why I am here. My expansion is my main source of wonder, and personal fulfilment. I am applying this to my business as well. I am more and more committed to saying 'no' to suffering every single day, for it is a choice.

As my journey of transformation continues to advance personally, I have been able to look back at my business career and see why transformation came so readily to me. I was definitely more evolved in a business context than I was in my personal life, and it reflected in my achievements in both walks of life. I was, and remain, imperfect in all parts of my life, but it doesn't matter because I am growing, and that is what matters to me most in the end.

I am but a microcosm of the macrocosm, which is the organism we call society. Our society, comprised of different collectives, is imperfect and flawed, and always will be. There is much that could be better, or more harmonious, and this is where our natural desire for 'more' can be redirected with great effect through more self-aware leadership.

For some, the orchestra is playing a Mozart classic, but for others the sounds are out of tune. We need evolved leaders to be our conscious conductors, bringing it all together in a harmony we can all feel and love.

It's fascinating that we continue to resist what is possible on an individual and collective level. We are what we choose to be, and our choices are determined by our level of self-awareness. The more we discover about our truths, the more we can become, and the closer we can move to being our loving true selves. Why would we be happy with anything less? The answer lies simply in the limits of our awareness.

The potential here is asymmetrical. Our upside is unlimited, because that is the very nature of our truth, as it reflects the nature of the ever-expanding universe of which we are a part. Our downside could get worse that's for sure, but for many people this is difficult to conceive, because they are already in a difficult place. Obviously, the asymmetry applies differently to all, depending on their circumstances. Only one thing is for sure, which is that our lives will change. It's up to us to make sure that that change is refreshing and positive for all. In many areas we need exponential growth, not just incremental improvement, or a constant restatement of what we see as normal.

My dream in *Where Your Happiness Hides* was to show the reader how transformation can apply on an individual level. Happiness springs forth when people are immersed in their unique truths and can then express that in unity with others, without harsh judgement. The ripple effect of human happiness, once sensed in enough individuals, can spread like the waves on the sea, and this was my dream in writing *Show Me The Harmony*.

We need leaders who are deep in self-awareness to create the waves of change, and ensure those waves land without fury on golden sands for the good of all. If a collective is like a jagged outcrop of rocks, the waves of change created within will crash and splash upon the shore, without harmony being present or possible. We thus need leaders who are in touch with their own hearts to lead the journey of evolution. From this place, transformation will gather pace.

The higher our collective consciousness then goes, the more by definition it will align with the journey back to love. Peace and unity will not be found in fear, because in this energy we will remain mired in our search for validation outside the realms of our inner craving for harmony and joy. We are all unique, but we need each other to come together in harmony to create a truly cohesive world – societies, governments, communities, companies and families alike. We truly need each other to share the resources on this planet for the benefit of all.

There is a big difference between contact and connection. Ever improving technology has increased our opportunity for contact, but through our hearts is the only true way to loving connection.

We must forgive those who have contributed to where we are now, for blame blocks the transmission of loving awareness; and together we must move forward with excitement, fascination, and a sense of hope for what will be possible.

This is possible with the right leaders – those evolved leaders I have described in this book. Leaders who can instil purity of purpose in collectives, who can conceive of the future, and have the presence to allow new possibilities to spring forth. They are the shepherds who will stand tall in their own self-knowing, who are committed to awareness and integrated in care, compassion, truth, and love, for they know the power of these energies over competition and fear. They will have the insights and foresights to show us the way to a world with less suffering.

May the leaders who fit this job description please step forward. Your heart will no doubt tell you that you can be an ambassador for the more loving experience we all deserve. Trust this message when it comes, and step into a new paradigm that you can help to shape. Our collectives need great transformation from the normal to a more natural way of operating, and you can have the great privilege of showing others this new way of being. May inclusion descend where exclusion once dominated our lives, for the benefit of all – not just the fortunate few. Show me the harmony, not just the money, for here is where true inspiration takes centre stage.

This can be truly transformational. I can already sense it appearing, without a shadow of a doubt in my mind!

May greater harmony rule our lives, for in its kingdom we will find great peace, abundance and happiness, together. That is my dream. I hope it's now yours!

# APPENDIX I

# Checklist for Evolving Leaders

Evolved leaders may choose to consider the following matters as they create our future collectives:

### Leadership Intentions

- Why do you want to lead others? What is your real motivation? It should be to add potency to a situation, or to help the common good; not 'to be important'.
- Do you see leadership as a specialist role requiring specific skills, or just an extension of a technical role?
- What matters more to you:
    - Your reputation?
    - Your integrity?
    - Your remuneration?
- How do you define success?
- What matters more to you – you, your people, or both?

## Integrity

- What does it mean to have integrity?
- Would you be prepared to lose your leadership role in the interests of self-love, integrity, and truth?
- What role does intuition play in your decision-making processes?
- To what extent do you trust your intuition over your thoughts? Do you suppress or dismiss your intuition?
- How readily can you admit to making a mistake?

## Balance

- Which do you consider to be more important in your decision making:
    - Profit
    - People
    - Purpose
    - the Planet (ie. the environment)
- What are your views on the importance of work/life balance?

## Truth

- Where do you stand on the importance of truth, rather than impression management?
- Would you be prepared to exit from your leadership role if it meant aligning with your integrity?
- How do you respond to a messenger bearing unpopular truths?
- What is the difference between honesty and integrity?
- Do you comprehend the difference between understanding a situation, and being in a place of knowing?
- Can you sense into energy to anticipate issues before they arise, or are you reactive only?
- How much energy do you expend on creating your image or protecting it, and why do you do this?

## Communication

- What do you believe are the key ingredients when communicating as a leader?
- Do you communicate with candour or spin?
- Are you truly open to receive upward and 360-degree feedback from others, then act upon it with integrity?
- Are you in contact with people, or in the space of deep connection with them?

## Well-being

- Where does the well-being of the people you lead and serve sit in your priorities?
- Could you put the well-being of others above your own, if you had to?
- As a leader would you invest significant money in the well-being of others?
- How do you honour your own well-being or the well-being of your family?

## Life

- What does it mean to you to be truly alive; not just secure or safe?
- How much do you value the life force all humans have? How does this influence the way you lead?

## Equality

- Do you really see everyone as equal in your team, or do you feel you have subconscious biases that you need to confront?
- Do you subscribe to the traditional hierarchical principles embodied in the pyramid structures collectives have typically deployed?
- Do you see the power of the sphere in collectives?

## Money

- How do you perceive the importance of money in your life and for the collective(s) you serve?
- How does money, and your share of it, impact on your ability to lead with integrity?
- Would you 'sell-out' your people if it meant your remuneration was increased significantly?
- Is your collective generating sustainable profits?

## Trust

- How do you create trust in the collective you lead?
- Do you understand the interrelationship between truth and trust?
- Do you truly trust yourself and your judgements?
- Do you trust those in your collective?
- Do you feel the need to check the work of others all the time?

## Purpose

- How much value do you place in your collective's purpose?
- How often do you reference purpose when you are making important decisions?
- How regularly do you communicate deep purpose to those you lead?

## Expansion

- Do you comprehend the importance of expansion to the collective you lead and the people within it, including yourself?
- Do you understand the intrinsic difference between expansion and inflation?
- Do you strive for inflation or expansion in your team, or for yourself?

## Self-Awareness

- How committed are you to your own self-awareness and the awareness of those you interact with?
- Do you invest enough resources in the development of your collective?
- What activities do you undertake in the interests of expanding your own levels of self-awareness?
- Do you really understand yourself and what you stand for?

## Emotions and Feelings

- Do you value and honour the importance of feelings and emotions in yourself and others that you interact with?
- How do you respond to emotions that may be foreign to your understanding?
- How do you show emotional vulnerability to your people?

## Heart-Based Decisions

- Would you say you lead with your heart or your mind, or both in unison?
- How empathetic and compassionate are you to people with lesser experience, effectiveness, or happiness?
- Does your collective seem to have a heart? Are your values aligned? If not, what actions could you consider resolving this misalignment?

## Vulnerability

- How open are you to being wrong?
- What do you do to show others that you are not perfect?

## Male/Female Energies

- Having read about male/female energies in this book, which ones are most dominant or subdued in you, and your collective?
- Do you plan to work on this mix?
- Will this principle change the way you recruit new leaders?

## The Golden Rule

- Do you really treat people the way you would like to be treated? If not, how can you approach this issue?

## Time v Energy

- Are you obsessed with time in your role? If so, where can you change your approach?
- Do you impose harsh/unnecessary deadlines to make yourself look good to your superiors?

## The Self

- Do you understand what is meant by being your true self?
- Would you say that you are self-centred, selfish, or selfless?

## Compassion v Assertiveness

- As a leader, where do you stand on the spectrum from compassion versus assertiveness? What drives this approach?
- Do you lead by creating healthy or unhealthy levels of competition between your people?

### Doing v Being

- As a leader how much do you do, versus delegate. Could you delegate more?
- Do you take enough time out to just be, so you can receive fresh inspiration?
- Do you ever meditate, or go to a place of peace, to connect more fully with yourself?

### Sight

- Which sight is your strongest?
    - Near-sight (seeing what is obvious)
    - Foresight (anticipating the future)
    - Insight (seeing new ideas)
- Do you strive to foster creativity in your collective, or focus on status quo maintenance?

### Unity v Separation

- What do you think creates greater outcomes for your collective – unity to foster collaboration, or separation to instil competition?
- How much value do you put in the power of unity to create?

### Decision-Making

- How quickly do you make decisions for your collective to move forward on?
- How much consensus or support do you need before making a meaningful decision?
- To make decisions do you rely mainly on gut feel, logic (including data, research, analysis) or a combination of both?
- Are you a people pleaser when you make decisions, or are you in a place of full integrity?

- Do you tend to make short-, medium- or long-term decisions? Is it balanced?
- To what extent do you listen to and consider fresh ideas from others in your collective before you decide?

### Innovation/Creativity

- How much of your collective is dedicated to developing new ideas, and continuous improvement?
- How do you oversee this?
- Do you give others due credit for their good ideas you inherit, or sell them as yours?

### Presence

- Do you talk more or listen more to others?
- When you meet with someone are you fully present?

### Fulfilment

- What constitutes fulfilment for you and your collective?
- How important is the happiness of you and your collective?

### Style

- Are you a shepherd, a wolf, or both depending on the leadership circumstances?
- Do you command respect or generate fear from those you interact with?

### Power

- Would you say you conduct power-play or powerful play?
- Do you use politics or integrity to create change?

- When needed, do you use your power to protect your collective from inappropriate criticism or treatment?
- Do you align with the powers of love and truth to create?

### Passion

- How passionate are you really about your role as a leader?
- Are there other career activities you would prefer to be involved in?

### Resilience

- How well do you deal with difficulties that arise?
- Do you see difficulties as disasters, or an opportunity for you and your collective to grow and develop?
- Do you try and cover up issues that arise, rather than deal with them with authenticity and integrity?

### Perfectionism

- Do you expect yourself, and others, to be perfect and fail to see learnings in these imperfections?
- How do you punish those, including you for making mistakes?
- Are you able to forgive people and/or find gratitude after mistakes are made?

### Role Models/Coaches

- Do you have role models or coaches who are helping you to grow as a person or leader, and who can really take you to the next level you are capable of?
- Who inspires you in life and why? What can you learn from them to help yourself and others?

## Fear/Needs

- What are your greatest fears in life?
- Which fears do you struggle most to let go of?
- What needs in your life do you feel are unfulfilled?

## Fun

- How much fun do you truly allow yourself when you interact with others?
- Do you think seriousness is needed to create success in the things you do?

# APPENDIX II

# 30 Mantras

The following mantras are useful reminders to help you re-train your mindset, should you wish to do so. They are also provided on my website at mark-worthington.com as a downloadable printable PDF, which you are welcome to print out and put somewhere accessible, to assist you in your personal transformation.

1. I feel first, then think, then act.

2. I never strive to be important, but rather to do important work.

3. My authenticity is the doorway to establishing trust with others.

4. My level of self-awareness determines what new possibilities can arise for me and my team.

5. An evolved leader creates through inclusion not exclusion, through collaboration not competition.

6. I strive to be more, not to own more, for here lies the inspiration my heart desires.

7. I will create better answers and outcomes for all by asking better and more incisive questions.

8. Contact is different to connection. Deep connection leads to the unity we all truly desire.

9. There is no room in my life for the blame game – failure provides me with opportunities to learn.

10. To be integrated is to have my heart, body and mind all in sync. In this way, I can access my natural intuition.

11. If I face fear with the respect it deserves, I can unlock great wisdom from which I can learn and expand.

12. I am the highest authority in my life, not the rules and views of others.

13. When I care for others and myself, I can care less about loyalty being present, for it will naturally arise.

14. My heart and mind are both incredible sources of intelligence. My body is the connector between these two great forces.

15. I can handle the truth, because to do otherwise is energetically expensive and will take me out of presence.

16. A problem is the gateway to higher awareness and rebirth in my life, and the lives of those I lead.

17. Nature teaches us that all must be rebalanced. Today I will look for greater balance in all that I am and all that I do.

18. Every day is an opportunity to reshape what success means to me and my team.

19. I stand for transformation, not just the accumulation of information.

20. Awareness, not data, is the gateway to new possibilities.

21. All begins as a dream, and manifests through the committed effort of teams of creative souls.

22. When I resist change, I invite mediocrity to persist in my life.

23. Opening up to new possibilities requires me to let go of all expectations, for they are the enemy of joy.

24. Wisdom can create money, but money will not create wisdom. Money is an energy of life but can never be its pure purpose.

25. The universe that opens my heart is my greatest teacher, not the university that taught me to think a certain way.

26. When I make peace with the views of all, I create power without the need for judgement and control.

27. When I operate with the pure intention in my heart, there is no need for perfection, for this place is perfect in its imperfection.

28. Deep purpose is found in truth and trust. Purpose established only in the mind can become no more than an illusion or source of hope.

29. I am the creator of my own destiny. What questions can I ask of creation today to expand my horizons?

30. Like the tallest oak tree, my team and I can only grow from where we are, not from where we hoped to be.

# APPENDIX III

## Our 22 Core Limiting Beliefs, Re-played

These are the 22 core limiting beliefs explored in detail in *Where Your Happiness Hides*. Together, these two interlinked books shed a light on the possibilities for individual and collective happiness and transformation.

### We Are Unworthy of Love

A core issue in our lives is that most of us do not love ourselves fully. Life has conditioned us to believe that we are unworthy of love, and therefore unworthy of the great happiness and abundance that life has in store for us, if we just believe in it.

### We Deserve to Suffer

For centuries, humankind has subconsciously believed that life is a struggle, and we all deserve to suffer. The world is difficult for many people, and as a collective this is partially the result of our inherent determination to embrace suffering.

### My Truth is the Truth

When we close our hearts and minds to the different views of others, we miss the opportunity to grow. There are facts and figures, but rarely is there one truth – for truth is just a matter of perspective and circumstance.

### There is a Lack of Resources

A basic underlying belief most of us share is that there is a lack of resources to go around, and only the winners get the spoils in life. Life has become based on competition, not collaboration, as we all seek to put ourselves above each other.

### We Live in the Past or Future

We are often not truly present in the circumstances in which we find ourselves. This is because our focus is often on the story of our past or our plans for the future.

### We Love with a Checklist

Love is a feeling, not a thought; yet we think our way through and into loving relationships.

### Money is Always Real and Unlimited

In our modern world, many governments have adopted what is known as Modern Monetary Theory. This is predicated on the view that money can be created and spent by governments at will to meet societal needs.

### We are Separate from Nature

As a race, humankind has lost touch with the reality that we are a part of nature, not separate from it.

## We Are Alone, Not All One

Humankind has rarely achieved great things through separation and segregation. Great ideas can spring forth from individuals, but to have collective benefit they need to be implemented in the spirit and energy of unity.

## Money Matters More than Love

Although we would all say love is more important in our lives than money, many of us do not live in alignment with this principle.

## We Must Reject and Fear the Feminine

To create a better world, we need a better balance of the male and female energies, after all it's what created all of us in the first place.

## Technology is Critical to Our Happiness

The use of technology in our society has reached epidemic proportions and,
    we suffer from information overload. But all this comes at the cost of transformation. Personal transformation can be far more powerful than information.

## We Don't Own Our Own Lives

Many of us give our lives away to make others happy, because we are conditioned to think that this is necessary for us to be loved and to survive.

## Our Bodies Don't Matter

Many people ignore their physical well-being and place it below other priorities in life, like money or work.

### Leadership Is Only About Getting Results

Our subconscious need to win has given us a propensity to promote people to leadership, normally men, who we believe can get results. Often, we do not care how they get results; we just care what they achieve.

### Life is a Random Event

As a society we believe that life is a great big random event. However, everything we encounter in life is a gift to us and has a purpose for us.

### Everything that Matters is Matter

Subconsciously as a society, many people only believe what they can see or touch.

### Change is Bad and Must be Avoided

Most people try to avoid change, for within change they perceive there lies the possibility of loss. Many people try to win by not losing, rather than by being extraordinary.

### Death is the End

The greatest fear of most human beings is the fear of death. With murders and wars always in the news, it's not hard to see why. This forces many of us to hide from possibility.

### Male and Female Energies are Totally Different

Our society stamps conditioned expectations on how men and women should live their lives.

How many people are living in a box that their heart really doesn't want them to be in?

### We Have the Right to Judge Others

Many people judge others as a way of elevating their own sense of worth. However, it is artificial, and not sustainable, and must be done constantly to make us feel more secure.

### We Are Humans Doing, Not Being

Many of us are validated by what we get done. To be busy and serious is to be needed and important. We have lost the ability to relax.

# Acknowledgements

Firstly, I would like to thank you, the reader. I am honoured that you have spent your valuable time (and money) considering the ideas I have put forward in this book, and I hope you have found them valuable.

If you are reading this book, you may have a strong interest in leadership, and/or a desire to enter the ranks of leadership, or perhaps you simply want to be led by those with more authenticity. Perhaps you have an inherent desire to make a difference in this often-troubled world.

I honour this commitment, and trust that this book can assist you along this important journey. Great leadership is critical to the creation of great collectives and great societies. Our world needs to evolve through more conscious leadership, and this means moving away from fear to love; for here lies the inspiration we crave. It's crucial.

The opportunity for transformation is ever present in our peripheral. We simply need to choose it for the benefit of all, and we choose it by embarking on a journey of truth and deep self-awareness. Self-awareness is the key to expansion and growth.

My special thanks go to the resolute team of people who have helped to bring this book into reality. I am humbled that the same team that helped me to create my book, *Where Your Happiness Hides*, have continued to support this book.

Andrea Gussy, my producer and co-ordinator, has again gone above and beyond to create this entire book from my handwritten manuscript. Her devotion to my cause is incredible.

Zena Shapter, my wonderful editor, has once again brought sparks to the pages to enhance the experience of my readers. Apart from her extraordinary skills with words, Zena brings a worldly and down-to-earth attitude to my team.

Bill Shapter, a gifted graphic artist and my internal diagram creator, has again done a wonderful job to bring greater expression to the words in this book.

Where would I be without Team Shapter?

Julia Kuris, my cover designer, created this book's beautiful cover and, in doing so, brought forth the calming feelings and emotions that harmony can create in a collective, led by wise and conscious leaders. I thank her for her wonderful design.

Mark Hunter, Charles Kovess and Sue Thompson have been powerful mentors in both my business and personal lives, and I acknowledge them for the many ways they have shaped my life for the better.

My special thanks also to Mark Hunter and David Reid, who gave up their valuable time to proofread this book for me.

I would also like to thank my family for their fantastic support during the creation of this book. They have always supported the passion I hope to bring to the world through the offerings in my books and my business.

Thank you all from my heart and mind.

May other hearts be set alight by the words in this book, and greater light be brought to those who are seeking to grow and improve their lives through the higher states of awareness that will inevitably follow.

# About the Author

Mark Worthington has lived most of his life in Sydney, Australia. He is the author of *Where Your Happiness Hides* (2022), *Show Me The Harmony* (2023), *From Pain to Possibility* (2024) and offers consultancy services and seminars to those seeking to transform their lives.

Mark has had a distinguished business career in a series of blue-chip organisations in both Australia and overseas. He was fortunate enough to work with some highly accomplished business executives, and lead some amazingly dedicated and talented people.

Mark was always fascinated with leadership, and wanted all who worked for and with him to feel their lives were better off because of their interactions with him.

Mark's career highlights so far have been based on the power of transformation and the importance of self-awareness. He was able to achieve incredible team transformations throughout his own 30yrs+ leadership career, without needing to change the people he inherited.

He did this with a powerful and often rare focus on people, and an unyielding commitment to truth, equality, and respect for those he led. His achievements are inspirational to those who wish to embark on a leadership career that is steeped in authenticity and truth. He has shown that truth is a flame that can improve the lives of a collective, for it burns inside their hearts, even if it is not expressed often enough.

Now in *Show Me The Harmony*, he brings forth his understanding of the power of love and truth to create greater happiness and success in human collectives of any kind. His consultancy business stands ready to assist any reader, or collective, interested in further understanding the book's concepts, and to apply them to their lives. To learn more, please visit mark-worthington.com or email Mark directly on mark@mark-worthington.com

www.ingramcontent.com/pod-product-compliance
Lightning Source LLC
Chambersburg PA
CBHW070803040426
42333CB00061B/1898